The Assets Agenda

Also by Rajiv Prabhakar

RETHINKING PUBLIC SERVICES
STAKEHOLDING AND NEW LABOUR

The Assets Agenda

Principles and Policy

Rajiv Prabhakar
London School of Economics, UK

First published 2008 by
PALGRAVE MACMILLAN
Houndmills, Basingstoke, Hampshire RG21 6XS and
175 Fifth Avenue, New York, N.Y. 10010
Companies and representatives throughout the world

PALGRAVE MACMILLAN is the global academic imprint of the Palgrave Macmillan division of St. Martin's Press, LLC and of Palgrave Macmillan Ltd. Macmillan® is a registered trademark in the United States, United Kingdom and other countries. Palgrave is a registered trademark in the European Union and other countries.

ISBN 13: 978–0–230–52219–0   hardback
ISBN 10: 0–230–52219–X   hardback

This book is printed on paper suitable for recycling and made from fully managed and sustained forest sources. Logging, pulping and manufacturing processes are expected to conform to the environmental regulations of the country of origin.

A catalogue record for this book is available from the British Library.

A catalogue record for this book is available from the Library of Congress.

10   9   8   7   6   5   4   3   2   1
17 16 15 14 13 12 11 10 09 08

Printed and bound in Great Britain by
CPI Antony Rowe, Chippenham and Eastbourne

To Sajiv

Contents

Acknowledgements

I have acquired a variety of debts during the writing of this book. This book is a direct result of an Economic and Social Research Council research fellowship on 'The Assets Agenda: principles and policy' (award reference RES 000–27–0164) at the Centre for Philosophy of Natural and Social Sciences at the London School of Economics. I am very grateful for the financial support received from the Economic and Social Research Council for this fellowship. Professor Keith Dowding acted as the mentor for this fellowship, and I am grateful for his advice and support throughout the fellowship.

The Centre for Philosophy of Natural and Social Sciences was a very supportive environment in which to work. I would particularly like to thank those connected with the Centre for all their help throughout the fellowship. Special thanks go to Stephan Hartmann and Eleonora Montuschi. I would also like to thank Miranda Lewis, Karen Rowlingson, Ian Shapiro and Stuart White for various discussions on some of the issues in this book. Karen Rowlingson deserves special mention for her detailed comments on the empirical chapters of this book. I have also benefited from seminars on asset-based welfare hosted by the Institute for Public Policy Research, as well as discussions held at Her Majesty's Treasury. Also valuable were presentations at the University of Bath, University of Birmingham, London School of Economics, Manchester Metropolitan University, University of Reading, and University of Sheffield.

I would like to thank my commissioning editor Philippa Grand at Palgrave Macmillan for all her support for this project. I would also like to thank Hazel Woodbridge at Palgrave Macmillan for all her help when I was preparing the delivery of the manuscript.

I would like to thank the editors of the *British Journal of Politics and International Relations* for permission in Chapter 4 to use material published in my article (forthcoming) on, 'Attitudes to the Child Trust Fund: what do parents think?'.

Finally, I am very grateful to my family and friends. I would like to thank my mother and father, my wife Helen and my children Maya and Arun for all the fun they provided. Thanks also to my friends during the course of this book: Ben Cowell, Preethike Dias, Cormac Hollingsworth, David Lingham and David Richardson. Finally, I dedicate this book to my brother Sajiv.

1
Introduction

This book looks at the assets agenda. In recent times the idea of spreading the individual ownership of assets such as capital grants, homes and savings has caught the imagination of politicians, academics and policy-makers in a number of places across the world. This interest surfaces in countries such as the United States, Canada, Australia, New Zealand and Britain. Implementing an assets agenda has potentially radical implications for the way that economic and social institutions are constituted. It points potentially to a radical redistribution of large inequalities of wealth that exists in many countries today.

Although there is a growing range of policy proposals and ideas for spreading individual assets, two key problems confront this agenda. First, the different ways that assets may be fashioned are often not clearly identified or considered. The assets agenda is composed of different strands. However, these currents are often conflated which tends to cloud rather than clarify debates. Second, there is a small evidence based on the ownership of assets. Although evidence on assets is growing, it remains fairly small. This hampers the formation of effective policy.

This book seeks to help remedy both of these defects. Thus I aim to add theoretical clarity and empirical evidence to current debates on the assets agenda. First, I identify and analyse two key themes informing the assets agenda. I distinguish between a strand that draws from political philosophy and concerns citizenship and a social policy current that connects asset-ownership to economic and social development. Second, I present original evidence on assets.

1

Original evidence is provided on one of the most prominent asset schemes in operation today, the British government's Child Trust Fund. I also provide evidence towards public attitudes on different ways of funding assets. A popular suggestion among supporters of assets is to use a wealth tax to fund assets. I present evidence on public opinion to wealth taxes.

Political interest

The assets agenda has provoked much interest in recent times. In the United States, George W. Bush made attempts to create an 'ownership society' a key part of his electoral platform in the 2004 presidential election. In a speech at the Republican party national convention in 2004 in which Bush accepted the Republican party nomination for president, he stated that, 'In an ownership society, more people will own their own health care plans, and have the confidence of owning a piece of their retirement ... We must strengthen Social Security by allowing younger workers to save some of their taxes in a personal account – a nest egg that you can call your own, and government can never take away'.[1] Bush outlines a series of ideas designed to promote his vision of an ownership society. Health Savings Accounts are tax-free savings accounts designed to help pay for health care expenses. Retirement Savings Accounts are tax free accounts intended to help saving for retirement, while Lifetime Savings Accounts are accounts that provide people with an opportunity to save tax free to help pay for education or training, the purchase of a first home, a car or retirement. Bush's interest added to the attention that President Bill Clinton paid to Universal Savings Accounts as part of his 1999 State of the Union Address. Clinton suggested using the surplus generated by the nation's finances to provide individuals with special savings accounts that would provide tax breaks for saving.

In New Zealand, Prime Minister Helen Clark stated in Parliament on 1 February 2005 that, 'Asset ownership is important for enabling people to participate fully in society. Assets provide people with greater security, control and independence' (Clark 2005). As part of this Clark supported schemes designed to help individuals save for their retirement as well as programmes intended to spread home ownership. In Australia, Mark Latham (2002), who became leader of the opposition Labor party in 2003, expressed his support for spreading individual ownership among the population. Drawing on a report published on behalf of the Chifley Research Centre (Allen Consulting Group 2003), Latham expresses support for Matched Savings Accounts.[2] These accounts provide matched contributions from public and private agencies for savings made by individuals.

In Britain, prominent politicians from the governing Labour party (Blunkett 2001; 2005; Milburn 2003) as well as the opposition Conservative party (Willetts 2002; Norman and Clark 2004) endorse a policy of spreading assets among the population. Former home secretary David Blunkett argues that owning an asset helps develop individual character and responsibility. He says that asset-holding offers, 'positive behavioural benefits. People who have a material stake in society are more likely to plan ahead for themselves and their children, and to care about what happens in the community around them' (Blunkett 2001, 34). On the basis of this, Blunkett supports initiatives such as the Child Trust Fund. More widely, he believes that asset-holding is important for progressive politics in the future.

Policy interest

The assets agenda stimulates interest among policy circles. In 2004, the World Economic Forum held a session at its annual meeting exploring 'Building the Investment State and the Ownership Society'. In this session delegates discussed how the individual ownership of financial assets could enhance the independence of those in poverty. The idea of providing people with capital grants was a particular topic of debate, and the British government's Child Trust Fund was considered as a concrete example of this approach. The session touched on issues such as the likelihood of such policies emerging in places such as the United States, how such policies should be funded and the role that financial institutions such as banks could play in backing such policies.[3]

Think-tanks and policy institutes are an important source of proposals on ownership. Bodies from across the world have developed a range of policy ideas, including the New America Foundation and the Cato Institute in the United States; Social and Enterprise Development Innovations in Canada; the Chifley Research Centre in Australia; and the Institute for Public Policy Research in Britain. In New Zealand, the think-tank the New Zealand Institute has made the individual ownership of assets central to its attempts to create an ownership society (Skilling 2004; Skilling 2005a; Skilling 2005b). The Chief Executive of the New Zealand Institute David Skilling writes that, 'Creating an ownership society, in which ownership of assets is broadly distributed through the population and in which all people are able to accumulate wealth over their lifetimes, is a policy priority across many countries' (Skilling 2005a, foreword). Skilling argues that although owning an asset is important for providing individuals with security, control and independence, a substantial portion of New Zealand's population do not have adequate assets to assets. Skilling proposes to counter this with a series of policies to spread individual ownership. The centrepiece of these proposals is a Kiwi Savings Account. These would be lifetime savings accounts that would be provided by birth. Government would give all newborns a $500 endowment at birth, and make additional $500 payments at ages five and ten. The government would also match any savings put into the account up to an annual limit of $500 for a period of 18 years.

When people enter the workforce, government would make a yearly contribution into the Kiwi Savings Account that amounts a 2 per cent cut in the personal tax rate faced by individuals. People would be required initially to save this tax-cut in the account. Government would also match any additional contributions people make at a rate of 0.5:1 and up to a limit of $1,000 each year. Those individuals in the lowest tax bracket, earning less than $38,000 per year, would have a higher 1:1 match. Money from the Kiwi Saver would be used for four specified purposes, namely paying for education, putting down a deposit on home, paying for retirement, or transferring to other family members.

In Sweden, asset-based policies have been discussed as a way of improving the country's system of social insurance (Fölster 2001; Fölster, Gidehag; Orszag, and Snower 2003). Stefan Fölster (2001) argues that the social insurance system in Sweden performs two main functions. First, it protects people against immediate risks such as unemployment. This protection usually involves redistribution between people, transferring resources from the better-off to the less well-off. Second, to help each person redistribute income over their own lifetime. Thus people can smooth income over their lifecycle, transferring money from their less needy to more needy periods, such as from their working life to their retirement. Fölster argues that a recent insight of economic research is that lifetime income is much more equally distributed than annual income. He continues that in Sweden the bulk of welfare expenditure focuses on lifecycle redistribution rather than redistributing between people in any given year. He says that 75–80 per cent of welfare expenditure goes to lifecycle redistribution, while the remaining 20–25 per cent redistribute resources between people. Fölster argues that personal savings accounts can help improve social insurance by freeing-up tax revenues currently dedicated to lifecycle redistribution and directing this to making annual incomes more equal.

Fölster highlights an education savings account as an example of this approach. He notes that the private insurer Skandia manages a voluntary learning account scheme that operates in around 50 companies in Sweden. Each employee can choose to put between 1 and 5 per cent of their salary into a learning account and this employee contribution is then matched by the employer. Savings can be used to pay for training, although an employer can retain its contribution for training that is deemed to go beyond the firm's needs. Funds in the account that are not spent are paid out in retirement or if a worker leaves the company, although the employer contribution is then returned to the firm. If a worker is made redundant then they keep both the employee and employer contribution. Stefan Fölster, Robert Gidehag, Mike Orszag and Dennis Snower (2003) argue that a general system of welfare accounts could improve the Swedish welfare system. Individuals would be required to save a minimum amount into these accounts, with the option of making additional savings if they wish.

In Chile, assets play a role in the pensions system. José Piñera (1996) notes that in 1981 workers were given a choice of taking out a Pension Saving Account (PSA) or remaining in the government run system. Under the PSA system, workers and employers do not pay a social security tax to the state. During their working life, the employee has 10 per cent of their wage placed automatically in their PSA. In 1996, this percentage was mandatory for the first $22,000 of yearly income. Beyond this level, workers are allowed to make additional voluntary contributions into their PSA. Individuals then have to place their account in one of a range of pension fund administration companies within the private sector. These companies invest the pension funds on the stock market. Piñera reports that in 1995, roughly a third of Chileans owned PSAs and that the $25 billion was contained in investment funds in a country whose gross domestic product was $60 billion.

Helen Barnard and Nick Pettigrew (2003) put forward an initiative for developing stakes in housing in policy work done for the Office of the Deputy Prime Minister in Britain. Housing equity schemes aim to allow people who face difficulty in buying a home to gain a stake or partial ownership in a property. Barnard and Pettigrew highlight a share and asset account version of housing equity schemes. In a share model, a person is provided with a direct share in a property. They say that residents of a housing association might be provided with a 1 per cent share in their home. If they adhere to their tenancy agreement (for example, pay the rent on time, do not be a nuisance to neighbours), then they may be provided with a further 1 per cent in their home each year. Residents may be able to purchase additional shares in their property. They can use shares as security for borrowing money, or sell their shares to raise money. If a person moves to another housing association, then they can use their shares to buy shares in their new home. Alternatively, if they move to the private sector, they can cash in their shares they have in their existing home. In an asset account model, a person is provided with a savings account that is run by their landlord. People will gain 'rental miles for the duration of their tenancy. Barnard and Pettigrew say that after a year a person may qualify for £500, and that people may receive rewards for keeping to their tenancy agreement and purchase extra miles should they wish. As savings grow, an account holder can use this to buy a share in their property or use this to put down a deposit on a home.[4]

Academic interest

Capital grants

Within the academy, Bruce Ackerman and Anne Alstott wrote *The Stakeholder Society* in 1999 which put forward an ambitious and eye-catching scheme to pay all United States citizens an $80,000 grant once they turn 21 years of age. Young people would be able to spend their grant however they please, with no strings or conditions attached to how the grant is used. Ackerman and Alstott proposed that a wealth tax could be used to help start up the stakeholder grant, and that eventually a move would be made to a largely self-financing system in which each generation of stakeholders would help fund the next generation of stakeholders by contributing to a central fund at the end of their lives. Their book has been the subject of extensive academic commentary. This proposal was an important focus for discussion at a recent conference on rethinking distribution at the University of Wisconsin in 2002, and the various contributions helped feed into a special issue of the journal *Politics and Society* in 2004 and a book within the Real Utopias project series edited by Erik Olin Wright (Ackerman, Alstott and Van Parijs 2005). Keith Dowding, Jurgen de Wispelaere and Stuart White (2003) also draw together a number of contributors that comment on various aspects of the Ackerman and Alstott scheme.

In Britain, Julian Le Grand and David Nissan (2000) put forward a similar scheme in the run up to the 2001 general election. As part of a series of pamphlets published by the centre-left think-tank the Fabian Society to provide policy ideas for a possible second term Labour administration, Julian Le Grand and David Nissan built on the idea of a 'demogrant' floated by Julian Le Grand in the late 1980s (Le Grand 1989) to advocate paying all young people a £10,000 grant once they reach 18 years of age.[5] Le Grand and Nissan propose a tax on inherited wealth to help pay for the grant. Unlike the Ackerman and Alstott scheme, however, Le Grand and Nissan argue that the grant should only be used for specified purposes, namely starting a business, paying for education or training, or buying a home.

Personal accounts

Michael Sherraden (1991; 2002) goes beyond capital grants in his proposals for Individual Development Accounts (IDAs). Sherraden says that IDAs are individual accounts that would be made available in the United States, and they would be tied specifically to purposes that were thought to advance personal and national development. IDAs deposits would be subsidised for poor families (though the subsidy would never provide the whole of the deposit) These funds would come from government. Individuals would have a range of choices over where to invest their IDA, and because IDAs are intended for long-term projects and goals, many schemes would be targeted at the young. Deposits would qualify for beneficial tax treatment, but if funds are withdrawn and not used for specified purposed then all subsidised funds would revert to the government. In addition, a substantial financial penalty would be levied on the individual. A parent or guardian would be allowed to transfer their IDA to their children or grandchildren.

Sherraden says that educational IDAs are an example of this generic policy model. These are IDAs that are designed to promote participation in post-secondary education. These accounts would be opened at birth, and deposits would be tied to various stages in the account holder's life. A $1,000 deposit would be allowed for at birth, and $500 could be placed in the account for each completed year of primary and secondary education. High school graduation would permit people to have a deposit of up to $2,500. A year of civic or military service might qualify for a deposit of $5,000. A sliding scale would be implemented, whereby poor families qualify for federal subsidies of up to 90 per cent of deposited funds, while rich families have to bear the full costs of deposits. Businesses and pupil fund-raising activities would be encouraged to add to the fund. Young people would be provided with information about their IDA at an early stage, with financial planning lessons integrated into the schools' curriculum. All funds would be tax-exempt if used for education or training, or to pay for expenses for these activities (such as childcare). Withdrawals would only be allowed once a person turns 18, or graduates from high-school (whichever is sooner), and between 18 and 35 years of age IDAs can only be used for education or training. After 35, people can transfer their IDA to their offspring. Alternatively, people can disband their IDA after 35. If they do so, then they would only receive their deposited funds plus the earnings on these deposits minus a 10 per cent financial penalty. The remaining money will go to government.

Anne Alstott (2004) outlines an asset scheme designed to help parents bring up their children. Alstott argues that child-rearing is one of the most life-changing of all human experiences. Alstott characterises parenthood as a 'no-exit' relationship, which means that there is a societal expectation that parents will provide long-term continuity care – at least 18 years – in nurturing their child's development from which parents cannot exit. She argues that there is often a tension between the needs of parents and children, with parents, especially women, having to make sacrifices (in terms for example of foregone promotion prospects in work) in order to look after their child. She argues that it is important to balance the needs of children and parents.

To help parents she advocates providing each of them with a Caretaker Resource Account. She refers to caretakers in recognition of the fact that those other than the biological parents might provide long-term continuous care for children. Individuals would receive an annual $5,000 grant that could be used for any of three specified purposes: childcare, the parents' own education, and the retirement of parents. Alstott notes that parents may have to deal with unexpected circumstances that impair their ability to look after their children, such as personal illness, and so Caretaker Resource Accounts should go hand-in-hand with a system of lifeplanning insurance which would be a public programme providing employment leave, income support and institutional assistance in times of difficulty.

Alstott advocates making these accounts available to all individuals. She favours a universal scheme for three main reasons. First, while in principle she has no objection to these accounts being 'opportunity tested', so that they are only made available for those whose opportunities fall bellow a certain level. She suggests that problems in measuring opportunities makes this option difficult to implement. Second, universal schemes are simpler and cheaper to administer than targeted initiatives. Third, a universal programme is likely to garner more popular support than a more limited measure.

Forerunners

Spreading individual ownership is not a new idea. Its roots can be traced at least back to the 18th century, informing the writings of figures such as Thomas Paine (1987) and Thomas Jefferson (Appleby and Ball 1999). Paine is probably the most celebrated forerunner of a programme of providing people with assets (Plender 1997; White 2003; Stedman-Jones 2004). Paine's ideas are set out most fully in his pamphlet *Agrarian Justice*. In this pamphlet Paine starts by making a distinction between the state of nature and civilisation.

The natural state is the earth in its uncultivated state, while civilisation arises when the world is cultivated by human activity. Paine argues that in the natural state the earth is common property. Paine contends that the natural state of the world would not have been enough to sustain human population growth, and while this necessitates a transition to civilisation, no one should be made worse off under civilisation than under the state of nature. While Paine accepts that people are entitled to reap the product of their labours, he says that individuals cannot disabuse others of their natural inheritance. He continues, however, that the system of landed property that has arisen in the modern world has dispossessed others, violating the principle that no one should be worse off under civilisation. To rectify this he puts forward a scheme to compensate individuals for their loss. He advocates creating a national fund that will pay everyone £15 once they reach 21 years of age. In addition, after the age of 50 he supports paying people an annual income of £10. He says that these payments should be made to rich and poor alike. In setting out this scheme he insists that it is, 'justice, not charity, that is the principle of the plan' (Paine 1987, 483). To pay for the plan, Paine makes a link to a tax on inheritance. He says that this is the best way of subtracting from property that part of it that is composed of natural inheritance.

John Cunliffe and Guido Erreygers (2004) argue that the ideas of Thomas Paine and Thomas Jefferson fed into 19th century political thought in the United States. Cunliffe and Errygers consider how the proposals put forward by Paine and Jefferson informed the thinking of commentators such as Cornelius Blatchly, Thomas Skidmore and Orestes Brownson. Cunliffe and Errygers argue that these later figures all stressed the importance of individuals having equal starts in life, but that the unequal distribution of wealth undermined the presence of equal starts. Blatchly, Skidmore and Brownson proposed changes in the system of inheritance to equalise the distribution of individual wealth. For example, Thomas Skidmore advocated a system of annual dividends where all the property of those who died in a particular year is split equally among all new people entering adulthood that year.

John Cunliffe and Guido Erreygers (2003; 2004) say that proposals for a basic capital grant can also be detected in 19th century liberal socialist thought in Europe. They identify a Belgian tradition setting out basic capital proposals encompassing individuals such as François Huet, Paul Voituron, Napoleon De Keyser and Agathon De Potter. For example, Agathon De Potter advocates a basic capital scheme in *Social Economics* in 1874. De Potter argues that a lack of financial resources creates a situation where the rich can exploit the poor. In particular, the wealthy can force the poor to work and extract the gains from their labour. To avoid this, De Potter proposes paying all individuals a social dowry once they reach adulthood. He says that the collective ownership of land would be used to help pay for these grants.

Broadly speaking, the above thinkers belong to a progressive wing of politics. The ownership of assets has also attracted the attention of more conservative political commentators. For example, during the 20th century individual ownership forms an important part of Hilaire Belloc's support for 'distributivism' as well as Quintin Hogg's *The Case for Conservatism* published in 1947. Hilaire Belloc (1927) argues that the individual ownership of the means of production is important for individual freedom. He says that owning land or capital allows a person to pursue their own life plans, choosing when to exercise his or her energies. Belloc acknowledges that capitalism can undermine individual freedom, particularly where ownership is concentrated in the hands of the few not the many. He continues, however, that the socialist solution of exercising common ownership of the means of production does not improve matters. He says that under socialism any concentration of ownership merely passes from private to state hands. The result is the formation of the 'servile state' which means that the many are now required by law rather than private landlords to work for the few. Belloc argues that the way to escape the clutches of the servile state is to revive the 'distributive state' that characterised much of the period in the Middle Ages. In particular, in Britain in the 14th and 15th centuries, production was organised mainly around the guild, that is independent and small-scale trade or craft associations based in villages. He argues that to tackle the servile state the key is to reverse the process by which the distributive state came to be eroded.

Quintin Hogg argues that private property is an essential component of freedom. He says that the experience of owning property develops the character of the property-holder. Hogg adds that private ownership is also important as it acts as a bulwark against state control. He says that the general benefits of private ownership mean that Conservatives are committed to creating a property-owning democracy. He writes that, 'According to Conservatives, the aim of every man may legitimately include the possession of enough private property to own, if he desires it, a house and a garden, to bring up a family including the provision of a slightly better education than the table d'hôte offered by the State, to indulge a reasonable hobby or leisure time occupation, and to end in his old age with a little more than the State pension, however generous ... We may be a long way off it, but this is the ideal – a "property-owning democracy" – which Conservatives hold' (Hogg 1947, 99–100).

Renewed interest

The assets agenda is an old idea that is being repackaged for new times. Current interest derives in important part from two sources. First, a desire to craft new agendas on ownership (Kelly and Gamble 1996; Paxton, White and Maxwell 2006). For much of the 20th century debates about ownership have centred on the merits of private versus common ownership. Common ownership was usually associated with the state. Of course, as seen above, there were figures who did not fall into this general pattern. Although debates about ownership did not focus only on private versus state ownership, it was nevertheless the case, much of the debate about ownership tried to weigh up the merits of private versus state ownership. Towards the end of the 20th century, the faith in state ownership began to wane. The problems encountered by state-owned enterprises during the 1970s as well as the failures of state socialism in the former Soviet Union and Eastern Europe during the late 1980s and early 1990s help contribute towards this loss of faith in state ownership.

Dissatisfaction with state ownership created a space in which different ownership agendas emerged. One strand of this looked at developing forms of common ownership that differed from state ownership. A different set of debates focused on developing different types of private property. Gavin Kelly and Andrew Gamble (1996) argue that historically the left had often neglected to explore the different ways that private property could be constituted. They contend that this failure to engage with private property meant that this terrain was ceded to the political right. The right was then allowed to set the terms of the debate about private property. Kelly and Gamble say that private property is too important to be left to develop in this way. They argue that the left should open up debates about the way that private property should be constituted.

The experience of 'popular capitalism' in places such as Britain provided an impulse for this rethinking (Plender 1997; Ackerman and Alstott 1999). Bruce Ackerman and Anne Alstott comment that when Margaret Thatcher was elected Prime Minister in 1979, '32 per cent of all housing was publicly owned. Although bent on sweeping privatization, Thatcher refused to sell off these vast properties to big companies. She invited residents to buy their homes at bargain rates. With a single stroke she created a new property-owning citizenry, and she won vast popularity in the process' (Ackerman and Alstott 1999, 12). During the 1980s, the Conservative government under Margaret Thatcher sought to create a property-owning democracy through policies such as widening share and home ownership. Nationalised utilities such as telecommunications and gas were privatised and council tenants were given the right to buy their flat or house they were living in. Reformists were drawn to this popular capitalism. They criticised Conservative policy, however, for not going far enough. It was suggested that the Conservative version of popular capitalism favoured the well-off and did not guarantee ownership for all. Efforts began to draw up proposals to create ownership for all. This fed contemporary interest in the assets agenda (Kelly and Lissauer 2000).

Second, an exploration of new directions in welfare or social policy (Haveman 1988; Sherraden 1991; 2003; Giddens 1998). Michael Sherraden states that, 'In the early 21st century the welfare state appears to be in the midst of a transformation' (Sherraden 2003, 28). During the 20th century, the state has played an important role in the funding and delivery of public and social services (Le Grand 2003). During the closing decades of the last century and the opening part of the 21st century the role of the state is being rethought. This rethinking is the result of a series of developments, which relate to things such as the impact of globalisation, rising costs of providing services wrought by technological change and an ageing of the population, heightened public expectations of the services they experience and theoretical criticisms of the state by 'New Right' political thinkers (Blank and Barau 2004; Prabhakar 2006). These factors have led to efforts to 're-state' the state (Gamble and Wright 2004).

One theme that has arisen as part of this rethinking connects to the concept of the social investment state. Sherraden points to the, 'emergence of 'social investment' as a dominant policy theme' (Sherraden 2003, 28). Instead of being the direct funder and provider of services, growing attention is paid to how the state might invest in individuals and communities to help themselves. One investment strategy that attracts attention is the state providing people with a range of individual assets or stakes to help themselves. For example, Robert Haveman (1988) argues for a new approach to securing equal opportunity and overcoming poverty. Haveman argues that equality should be a key aim of public policy, and that equality should be understood in terms of the provision of equal opportunity. This means that public policy should ensure that people are able to start life from an even or level position in terms of the opportunities open to them. Haveman argues that social policy in the United States has failed to guarantee that people 'start even'. He says that particularly since the 1970s, an assumption has spread among political circles that government policies on redistribution are harmful for efficiency. He says that this presumption of a trade-off between equality and efficiency has had two important consequences for the fight against inequality and poverty. First, it creates a pressure for a retrenchment in welfare services. The view that government programmes on poverty and inequality will lead to losses of efficiency is used as an argument to curtail welfare services. Second, the equality-efficiency trade-off has stopped policy-makers from thinking about the innovative policies that are needed to tackle new social problems. Havemen says that new inequalities have arisen in relation to particular groups within society, such as lone parents and youths from minority communities. Haveman contends that the mindset of equality versus efficiency has prevented an exploration of how these new inequalities can be addressed.

Haveman challenges the assumption of a trade-off between equality and efficiency. He says that inequality is detrimental to efficiency, and so improvements in equality will also enhance efficiency. He says that breaking out of this mentality creates a space in which different types of policy intervention can be explored and considered. He states that existing policies towards inequality have often relied on income transfers. He continues that these income transfers do not resolve problems, however, as they do not attack underlying problems of dependency. People simply become dependent on income transfers and do not take preventative measures to avoid problems in the first place. Haveman argues that policy should focus on investing in people so that they become independent and break out from a cycle of dependency. He writes that, 'strategies for taxing and transferring income requires continual government intervention for the gains to be sustained. There is nothing inherent in them to enable recipients to become more self-sufficient, to assure their independence by their own efforts. Long-term and permanent progress against poverty and inequality is possible only through programs that make it possible for individuals to acquire sufficient skills and training to become economically independent, and give them incentives and hope to make the effort' (Haveman 1988, 23). Haveman advocates a range of policies to provide this independence. One type of policy concentrates on providing people with stakes. For example, he supports a capital grant for young people. He proposes paying a $20,000 grant to all individuals when they turn 18. The grant would only be used for approved purposes, which he says would primarily be for paying for education or medical care. Education and health are seen as important for guaranteeing individual independence, and having healthy and educated individuals is seen as important for efficiency. Haveman argues that encouraging people to make decisions about health and education should also foster a sense of individual responsibility.

Policy examples

In terms of actual policy, there are a number of initiatives that are implemented or at the pilot stage in different parts of the world. Perhaps the most prominent national scheme is the British government's Child Trust Fund. This policy pays all babies born from September 2002 a capital grant from government. There are currently around 700,000 babies born in Britain each year, and so the

Child Trust Fund is provided to large numbers of newborns. Babies from families whose household income is less than approximately £13,000 per year receive £500, while remaining babies receive £250. The Child Trust Fund has to be placed into a special account that matures once the child is 18 years old. The account-holder, family and friends can contribute up to £1,200 per year into these accounts. Once the fund matures after 18 years the young person is free to spend their Child Trust Fund however they please. During the lifetime of the account, the child will receive lessons at school on how to manage their Child Trust Fund (Her Majesty's Treasury 2003). The government has recently announced that there will be additional £250 or £500 top-ups placed into the account when the child is seven (His Majesty's Treasury 2006).

Although the account is in the child's name, parents or guardians are responsible initially for choosing the type of account within which to invest the Child Trust Fund. Providers are banks or building societies on the high street. Three main types of accounts are available. First, an interest bearing deposit account. These are standard savings accounts which tend to promise a particular rate of return. Second, a share account. This invests the Child Trust Fund in shares on the stock market. This offers the prospect of higher risk but higher returns than the deposit account. Third, stakeholder accounts. These also invest funds in shares, but as the account approaches maturity money is shifted into lower risk investments. If a parent or guardian fails to open a Child Trust Fund on behalf of their child, the Inland Revenue will open up a stakeholder account for the child (www.childtrustfund.gov.uk, accessed on 13/12/05).

On a smaller scale, Individual Development Accounts are available in 34 states in the United States as well as Washington D.C. and Puerto Rico. As of January 2003, 500 Individual Development Account initiatives covering at least 10,000 individuals. A federal Assets for Independence Act passed in 1998 is expected to provide between 30,000 and 40,000 extra participants in Individual Development Account schemes, drawn mainly from the ranks of the working poor (gwbweb.wustl.edu/csd/Areas_Work/Asset_building/IDAs/, accessed on 13/12/05).

There are also a number of initiatives at the pilot stage. For example, educational assets are currently being investigated in Canada. A *learn$ave* scheme is operating at the following ten sites:

Vancouver, Toronto, Halifax, Calgary, Winnipeg, Greg-Bruce counties (Ontario), Kitchener-Waterloo, Montreal, Fredericton and Digby (Nova Scotia). The Social Research and Demonstration Corporation and Social and Enterprise Development Innovations is conducting this project which was launched in June 2001 and due to last until June 2009. It is being funded by Human Resources and Skills Development Canada, and 4,827 participants enrolled in the programme between June 2001 and the closing date of December 2003. The *learn$ave* project is designed to help low income individuals save money in order to boost their human capital. Under the initiative, the programme contributes $3 for every $1 that is saved by a participant. Account holders have up to 3 years to save a maximum of $1,500, and so with matching contributions the total amount saved can amount to $6,000. Following the 3-year period individuals have one more year to spend their savings and matched funds. The savings can be used to purchase training courses or small business start-ups. Setting up a small business is allowed because it is assumed that this will enhance the skills of account holders. As part of the scheme, financial management training and case management support is provided to programme participants.

Criticisms and challenges

The assets agenda provokes critical commentary as well as support among the academic, policy and political community. Questions have been raised about the extent to which assets are able to achieve their stated policy objectives. One of the objectives of policies such as the Child Trust Fund, Matched Savings Accounts and Individual Development Accounts is to encourage people to save or accumulate further assets, particularly among the 'asset-poor' who have few assets or savings. Some observers claim, however, that it is precisely this target group of the asset-poor that are in no financial position to save. The asset-poor face financial struggles in making ends meet and so cannot save. In fact the only people who will be able to save are those that are already 'asset-rich'. In his role as the head of the Child Poverty Action Group in Britain, Martin Barnes writes that, 'Supporters of asset-based policies claim that the poor can save. Many find this counter intuitive. It invites the response: 'If they can afford to save, can they be poor? The assertion may also surprise the half of lone parents on income support who also lack sufficient income to provide necessities for their children' (Barnes 2002, 14).

Carl Emmerson and Matthew Wakefield (2001) say it is important to ask whether asset-ownership constitutes the *best* way of attaining these objectives. This viewpoint insists that to command support, it is not enough to demonstrate that asset-ownership will achieve their stated targets. It must also be demonstrated that asset-ownership is preferable to alternative policy tools. This is important to ensure the best use of available resources. For low-income adults, an obvious alternative to asset-based welfare is to rely on additional income supplements. Alternatively, money allocated to assets might be used instead to increase spending on public services, for example in boosting 'early years' or primary education provision. Carl Emmerson and Mathew Wakefield question whether the money spent on assets as a way of improving financial education might not be better directed at providing extra classes at schools, colleges or the workplace.

Public opinion is likely to impose a series of challenges that policy-makers need to confront. The sustainability of any policy depends on the support it receives from the public. Public support is needed to help ensure that people co-operate with the policy and do not put pressure on elected officials to remove the policy. Public opinion is likely to give rise to constraints affecting initiatives such as capital grants, affecting both the forms that stakes take as well as how they are funded. We have seen above that one important difference between the grant proposals put forward by Bruce Ackerman, Anne Alstott, Julian Le Grand and David Nissan relates to whether or not conditions or restrictions are imposed on how grants are used. One of the dangers facing a policy that does not place restrictions on how a grant is used is that public support may wane with well-publicised cases of individuals 'blowing' their stakes. Julian Le Grand states that there could be, 'no surer way to lose popular and political support for a system of demogrants than a few well-publicised cases of young people blowing their stakes on cocaine or wild holidays' (Le Grand 2003, 129). The view that the public may desire that grants are only spent for particular 'useful' purposes receives some empirical support from a project conducted by Andrew Gamble and Rajiv Prabhakar (2006) on the attitudes of young people in England towards capital grants. Gamble and

Prabhakar convened focus groups with one of the main target groups for capital grant proposals, that is young people aged 18 years of age. Eleven focus groups were convened in two locations, and there were approximately eight participants in each group. The groups were used to explore the attitudes of young people to things such as what they thought of imposing restrictions on how capital grants are used. One of the findings of this research was that there was general support for using grants for specified purposes, and this emphasis on conditions became stronger as the size of the grant under discussion was increased. The most popular things that young people themselves said the grant should be spent on paying for education, buying a car, putting a deposit on a home or starting a business. The young people tended to support these conditions mainly on the grounds that any grants they received should be used in what they saw as a responsible fashion.

In relation to funding, one thread connecting different stakeholder proposals relates to an emphasis placed on using inheritance or wealth tax to fund stakes. There are grounds to suspect that the public is likely to exhibit resistance to the use of inheritance tax. Robert Goodin comments that, 'Inheritance taxes have long been the 'third rail' of tax policy: touch them, and you are dead, politically' (Goodin 2003, 70). Michael Graetz and Ian Shapiro (2005) provide an account of the way that a coalition of conservative commentators, linking together figures from the Republican party, small business and right-wing think-tanks, have succeeded in securing popular support for a repeal of inheritance tax in the United States, even though such a repeal would mainly benefit the very rich. Graetz and Shapiro say that an important part of this success lies in the way that conservative opponents of inheritance tax have manipulated the way that inheritance tax has been presented and debated among the wider public. For example, Graetz and Shapiro say that conservatives succeeded in branding inheritance tax in a negative fashion, dubbing it a 'death tax'. In addition, evocative case studies and stories have been advanced in the argument against the tax even though these stories misrepresent the politics of taxation. Graetz and Shapiro continue that failures in the way that supporters of inheritance tax presented their case also contributed to the lack of public support for this tax.

In Britain, Miranda Lewis and Stuart White (2006) conducted deliberative seminars in the north and south of England with

32 members of the public. Individuals were asked initially about their views on inheritance. The groups then heard arguments both for and against inheritance taxes from political theory, and the project explored whether people's attitudes changed as a result of discussions stimulated by expert witnesses. Lewis and White found that at the outset 16 believed that estates should not be taxed, one person was in favour of such a tax, 10 people stated it depends on the estate and five declared they did not know. At the end of the sessions, 16 people believed estates should not be taxed, nine thought that estates should be taxed, six said it depended on the estate and one stated they did not know. Lewis and White say that although support for inheritance tax rose during the session, it, 'must be acknowledged that at the end of the workshops there remains a clear majority of firm opponents of the principle of taxing inheritance over firm supporters of this principle' (Lewis and White 2006, 25).

Miranda Lewis and Stuart White (2006) confirm some of the findings of an earlier study of public attitudes towards inheritance taxes conducted by a Commission on Taxation and Citizenship (2000). In 1998, the centre-left think-tank the Fabian Society established a Commission to investigate the attitudes of the public in Britain to taxation. As part of this study, the Commission conducted a survey of members of the public about their general attitudes towards taxation. One thousand seven hundred and seventeen individuals aged 18 or over took part in the survey conducted between 19 June and 7 July 2000. The survey found substantial opposition to inheritance tax, with around half the people believing there should be no inheritance tax at all.

Problems

Two barriers exist in making progress on these issues. First, there is a lack of clarity at a theoretical level. The assets agenda is not a unified body of thought. Different wings can be identified within the broad assets agenda. Two strands are of particular importance, namely a 'social policy' and 'citizenship' mode of thinking. Within the field of citizenship, the ownership of assets is seen as a matter of justice. This means that justice demands that individuals have rights over particular resources, or assets are important for securing freedom. Within social policy, owning assets is viewed largely as a tool for achieving economic and social objectives. For its supporters, asset-ownership is thought to be important for promoting economic and social development. These citizenship and social policy traditions view assets in different terms. Within the citizenship arena, asset-holding would still be justified even if spreading individual ownership is harmful for economic or social development. Within social policy, however, if assets fail to foster economic or social development, then a large part of the case for asset-holding is undermined. Bruce Ackerman and Anne Alstott highlight the contrast between justice and economic and social objectives when they say that one of the most common objections to their scheme of providing $80,000 stakes to all 21 year olds is that this money would be better spent on other policies to tackle poverty. Ackerman and Alstott reply, however, that this objection misconstrues their proposal. They say that, 'Stakeholding is not a poverty program. It is a citizenship program' (Ackerman and Alstott 1999, 197).

The citizenship and social policy wings have different implications for the ownership society. For example, citizenship focuses on the rights and responsibilities of all members of a political community. This means that accounts of citizenship within the assets agenda are disposed towards universal schemes or initiatives. Social policy accounts focus on attaining particular economic and social policy goals. While the pursuit of these goals allows for the presence of universal schemes, it also has a greater space than citizenship for schemes that are targeted at particular sections of the population.

As will be seen in a later chapter the arguments used within the tradition of citizenship to provide a case for the provision of things such as capital grants also point to using some form of wealth tax to fund stakes. Within the social policy realm, broad arguments about the role of stakes in fostering economic and social development leaves open the issue of how stakes should be funded. While inheritance or wealth taxes might play a role, so might the use of other forms of taxation or cuts in public expenditure elsewhere. These other options for funding play a larger role within social policy than citizenship.

There is often a failure, however, to distinguish between these different agendas. Bruce Ackerman and Anne Alstott have already commented above that their $80,000 citizenship grant is frequently misjudged on social policy grounds. Elsewhere Carl Emmerson and Matthew Wakefield (2001) question whether policies such as the Child Trust Fund and Saving Gateway are the best way of achieving social policy goals. On the basis of this, they question the value of asset ownership. However, even if it is true that providing assets is not the best way of promoting a specific social policy goal, on its own this is not enough to reject the assets agenda. It might still be possible to justify the assets agenda as a desirable component of citizenship. A failure to separate out different strands to the assets agenda tends to cloud rather than illuminate discussions of assets.

Second, a lack of evidence about the effects of asset ownership. John Bynner comments that, 'Unlike the solid foundation of research into the effects of income on welfare outcomes, empirical research on the value of asset holding is rare' (Bynner 2001, 17). As we shall see later, some evidence does exist about the impact that owning assets has on things such as saving. The most extensive evidence comes from the United States, mainly in relation to a 4-year study conducted by the Center for Social Development at the University of Washington at St Louis (Sherraden 2002). The director of the Center for Social Development Michael Sherraden has led a team of researchers conducting a range of studies on Individual Development Accounts as part of a programme entitled the American Dream Demonstration. Elsewhere, there have been quantitative and qualitative studies conducted on assets by bodies such as the Institute of Education in London (Bynner 2001) and the Personal Finance Research Centre at the University of Bristol in England (Kempson, McKay and Collard 2005). Although empirical data does exist on assets, the evidence on assets is still fairly small. There is little data, for example, on the Child Trust Fund. It is important to add more data if 'evidence-based policymaking' is to be advanced.

Aim of this book

This book aims to help address the above shortcomings. In doing so, I seek to push debates about the assets agenda one step forward. The book aims to remedy the defects of the current situation in two main ways. First, I conduct an examination of each of these traditions, looking at the assumptions and arguments that inform each of the wings of the assets agenda. During this examination I scrutinise the differences that exist within as well as between different elements of the assets agenda. This covers issues such as whether or not restrictions are imposed on the use of assets, the various ways that stakes may be funded, and the relationship of assets to other policy instruments (for example, should stakes be conceived as a replacement for traditional forms of welfare support, or should stakes be designed to complement these other policies).

Second, I present original evidence on the assets agenda. Part of this sets out evidence on the British government's Child Trust Fund. The Child Trust Fund is worth studying for a variety of reasons. First, this provides direct evidence for similar proposals on an international stage. There is interest in implementing a similar policy in other countries, inspired in part by the example of the Child Trust Fund. Peter Nares, the founding executive director of Social and Enterprise Development Innovations in Canada, says that, 'It is time for Canada to build on our experience as well as that of the United States and the United Kingdom and begin developing policies and programs, such as the Child Trust Fund and IDAs, which help the asset poor' (Nares 2003). In the United States a Kids Investment Development (KIDS) account has won the backing of Democrat and Republican politicians. This proposal is part of an American Savings for Personal Investment, Retirement and Education (ASPIRE) programme and supporters in the Senate include Republican Rick Santorum and Democrat Jon Corzine and in the House of Representatives Democrat Pat Kennedy and Republican Phil English. The government would provide a $500 asset in a KIDS account for every child born after December 31 2006. Those babies in households below the national median income would qualify for an extra $500. Family and friends can save up to $2,000 (House bill) or £1,000 (Senate bill) into these accounts each year. These households below the national median income level would also be eligible for a dollar-for-dollar match for the first $1,000 (House bill) or $500 (Senate version) that they save into these accounts. Accounts would mature after 18 years, but the funds could only be used for education, buying a home or saving for retirement. When an account holder turns 30, they have to start paying back the initial endowment to government to help fund the next generation of KIDS accounts (www.AspireAct.org, accessed 6/2/07). An examination of the Child Trust Fund provides information that is directly relevant for such international measures.

Second, the Child Trust Fund is a concrete policy example. Asset initiatives are more advanced at the level of ideas rather than actual policy. The Child Trust Fund is noteworthy because it is an actual policy not just an idea. Proposals such as the KIDS accounts mentioned above is still at the stage of discussion rather than actual policy. The ASPIRE act was originally introduced at the 108th Congress, but was not acted upon. It was reintroduced at the 109th Congress in April 2005, though as of December 2006 it appears that it would not be enacted by the end of the 109th Congress.

Third, this adds value to existing studies of asset policies. Much of the available data relates to Individual Development Accounts in the United States, or related schemes such as the Saving Gateway in Britain. An examination of the Child Trust Fund adds to our current stock of empirical knowledge by looking at a different policy. The Child Trust Fund is also different from other policies because it is a universal measure. Individual Development Accounts do not at present apply across the whole of the United States. The Child Trust Fund does have universal coverage, and is interesting as a concrete example of a universal assets policy.

I present original evidence gained from discussions with parents who hold the Child Trust Fund. I explore parental reactions to different ways that the Child Trust Fund may be designed. Do parents like the grants for their children? Would parents prefer to receive additional income supplements instead of capital endowments for their children? Are parents concerned about the possibility of stakeblowing?

I also discuss different options for funding assets. Public opposition to inheritance taxes raises a challenge for the assets agenda given the emphasis placed on wealth taxes as a way of paying for assets. I ask whether wealth taxes can be framed or shaped in such a way that avoids or reduces public opposition. I also consider alternatives to wealth taxes. Part of this looks at public attitudes to a 'community fund idea' that creates a pot of money on behalf of the nation. Stuart White suggests that government could create a national fund, and money from this fund would be invested on the stock market by independent financial advisors. The returns to the investment would be used to help pay for capital grants (White 2003). The study of alternatives to wealth taxes also considers public attitudes to using cuts in public spending elsewhere (on things such as education and health) to pay for assets.

Chapter structure

Chapters 2 to 4 address the first theme of this book, namely the exploration of the theoretical background to the assets agenda. Chapter 2 is dedicated to the examination of social policy and Chapter 3 looks at citizenship. Models of social policy usually claim that owning an asset leads to changes in individual behaviour that benefits economic and social development. One class of models insists that changes in behaviour arise because of changes in an individual's character. This 'character development' approach suggests that assets have an 'asset effect' that causes them to think differently about the world. An alternative 'incentives' approach claims that changes in behaviour comes about because assets alters the balance of incentives faced by individuals. This chapter considers the main assumptions behind each approach as well as the differences that exist between these different viewpoints. The chapter then contemplates funding issues, looking at the different options suggested within the social policy tradition.

Chapter 3 turns to differences within the field of citizenship, underlining that different versions of the assets agenda exist within as well as between intellectual traditions. I make a distinction between those models of citizenship based on principles of just distribution and those versions founded upon a notion of a republican citizenry. I highlight differences over issues over whether or not restrictions are placed on how assets are used.

Models of citizenship usually advocate some form of wealth tax to pay for assets. An obvious way of guaranteeing ownership for all is to redistribute from the 'asset-rich' to the 'asset-poor' by taxing wealth. Wealth taxes can be shaped in a number of ways. This chapter canvasses the main options that are available, and link these to different models of citizenship.

Chapter 4 rounds off the examination of the theoretical background to the assets agenda by outlining the main policy differences that arise between the social policy and citizenship wings. A tentative suggestion is made for a hybrid approach that combines aspects of social policy and citizenship when crafting policy proposals.

Chapters 5 and 6 consider the second theme of the book, that is empirical evidence on the assets agenda. These chapters look respectively at issues of provision and funding. Chapter 5 presents original evidence on the attitudes towards stakes from parents who hold the new Child Trust Fund grants. This chapter examines the views of those who get the lower and higher endowments. The focus group discussions pursued two main themes. First, what were parental attitudes towards the Child Trust Fund as it currently stands. This examines attitudes towards basic features of this policy, such as the size of the endowment and its universal nature. Second, the study looks at alternatives to the current policy. Part of this explores attitudes to placing restrictions on the use of assets. In addition, parents were asked whether they would prefer money dedicated to the Child Trust Fund to be spent instead on higher income benefits or public services.

Chapter 6 provides evidence on attitudes to funding. This looks at two questions. First, what are public attitudes to wealth taxes? Do attitudes to inheritance tax change if arguments are couched more in terms of stories and case studies than statistics and facts? Also, does opposition dissipate when people are offered choices over the taxes they pay? Do they prefer to pay higher estate duties but lower income taxes to lower estate duties but higher income taxes? What do people think of land tax as a different way of raising money from wealth?

Second, what do people think about alternatives to wealth taxes? Part of this looks at public opinion towards the community fund idea described above. The remainder of this chapter contemplates attitudes to using cuts in public services elsewhere to pay for assets.

Chapter 7 provides a brief overview of the material covered in this book and considers the future prospects for this agenda. It notes that this agenda has emerged most strongly in the 'Anglo-Saxon' world encompassing the United States, Canada, Britain, Australia and New Zealand. I consider the view that this connection is not accidental but occurs because assets are an Anglo-Saxon policy. I reject this perspective, and argue that assets have the potential of being extended into the non-Anglo-Saxon world, particularly if this is built around the citizenship wing of the assets agenda. I finish off by suggesting directions for future research.

2
Social Policy

Introduction

This chapter examines the assets agenda within the area of social policy. This starts the task of exploring the theoretical background to asset-based policies. Arguably the main source of contemporary interest in assets comes from social policy thinking. Will Paxton comments that an, 'interesting recent public policy debate has centred on asset-based welfare. This approach is founded on the notion that the stocks of wealth that an individual holds and not just their income or consumption should be seen as important when assessing their wellbeing' (Paxton 2003, 1). Much of the debate about assets is conducted within social policy circles, occurring in bodies such as the Institute on Assets and Social Policy based at Brandeis University in the United States, Social and Development Innovations in Canada and the Institute for Public Policy Research in Britain. 'Asset-based welfare' is one of the most commonly used terms today to describe a policy of emphasising the individual ownership of assets such as savings, pensions or a grant. The term asset-based welfare was coined by Michael Sherraden (1991) at the turn of the 1990s to describe what he argued is a new direction in welfare policy in the United States. The name asset-based *welfare* indicates that this mode of thought has origins and applications within the area of social or welfare policy.

Asset-based welfare consists of different strands of thought. Thus, differences exist within social policy as well as between social policy and citizenship. In this chapter I identify two principal currents of thought feeding into asset-based welfare. First, and most importantly, a 'character development' approach that claims the ownership of assets helps develop individual character. This strand is the dominant approach in the current social policy literature and has its origins in the work of the American academic Michael Sherraden. The notion of an 'asset-effect' is central to this approach, namely the idea that owning assets causes people to think differently about the world. The second perspective is an incentives framework that says that owning assets alters the balance of incentives faced by individuals in ways that promote efficiency and productivity.

Both the character development and incentives approach suggest that owning assets alters behaviour. The character development strand believes ownership changes behaviour by developing character while the incentives framework takes each person as a given but proposes that asset-ownership alters behaviour by changing incentives. Andrew Dobson (2004) illustrates the difference between incentives and character development in a different field of study. He says that one way of trying to encourage people to protect the environment is to provide them with incentives as part of a contract. For instance, councils could impose financial penalties on those that do not separate out glass or paper for recycling as part of their weekly refuse. This approach takes each person's preferences as fixed and tries to change behaviour by changing incentives. Dobson says that the problem with this strategy is twofold. First, it may often be difficult to design incentives to achieve the desired effect. For instance, councils that charge people for every rubbish sack they deposit in an effort to minimise waste might find that they encourage fly tipping rather than the reduction in waste. Second, and more fundamentally, the desired behaviour disappears if incentives are removed. Dobson contends that even if incentives can resolve the design problem, if they are taken away then people will 'revert to type'. Dobson continues that a scheme of incentives will usually depend upon the support they receive from politicians, but this then makes incentives vulnerable to swings in political fashion. Changes in behaviour are not robust as incentives could be easily removed. Dobson argues that more long-lasting changes in behaviour are likely to result from moulding character, and specifically moral change within individuals, than treating preferences as fixed and trying to devise incentive schemes to promote particular types of behaviour.

The chapter proceeds as follows. First, I consider the main elements of the character development and incentives wings of asset-based welfare. I then examine some of the similarities and differences between the character development and incentives strands of the assets agenda. The chapter then moves on to consider the issue of funding. I finish off by looking at the relationship of assets to other aspects of welfare policy, in particular income benefits and public services.

Character development

A commitment to 'preventative welfare' provides the background to the character development approach. One approach to welfare is to try and cure problems once they have already arisen. This approach responds to problems such as poverty and unemployment as they arise and then steps are taken to try and overcome these problems. One of the main tools that have been used as part of this approach is income redistribution. This redistributes income from the better-off to the worse-off to try and alleviate social problems. Income redistribution is arguably the dominant tool used to address social policy problems for much of era after the end of the Second World War. Michael Sherraden comments that, 'To date, social policy for the poor has been focused almost entirely on income' (Sherraden 2003, 28).

An important part of the impetus behind asset-based social theory is driven by concerns with curative welfare. Julian Le Grand and David Nissan (2000) argue that one difficulty with curative policies is that they may encourage a culture of welfare dependency whereby individuals take few steps to avoid problems from emerging. Individuals come to expect that the state will always come to the rescue, and so curative welfare might actually perpetuate problems. In addition, they say that curative measures are politically unpopular because, building on the previous point, there is a perception among the public that people have only themselves to blame if they find themselves in adverse situations. Thus it is difficult to generate and sustain support for curative measures.[1]

Investment

Rather than trying to alleviate the effects of problems once they have already occurred, preventative welfare aims to stop problems from emerging in the first place. Investment is regarded as key to this preventative agenda. The idea is to encourage people to make investments that help stop problems from arising. For example, individuals may be able to avoid unemployment by making appropriate investments in education or training. This investment in education allows people to acquire skills that are attractive for current and future employers. Similarly, if individuals make the necessary savings, then they may be able to avoid poverty in retirement (Haveman 1988; Commission on Social Justice 1994; Sherraden 2003).

Investment can take a range of different forms. One type of investment concerns activities undertaken by collective organisations. For instance, in deprived neighbourhoods, government might establish organisations that comprise of representatives of local residents, businesses and public officials (such as local councillors). Government might provide these 'community development trusts' with financial resources dedicated to helping start-up local businesses, pay for schemes intended to improve the environment or set up clubs that allow people to network and exchange ideas about to tackle local problems. Community development trusts would then be charged with devising and implementing a series of investments within the community (Commission on Social Justice 1994).

A different set of investment strategies focus on providing resources to individuals. Asset-based welfare is an example of this type of investment. The idea is that providing people with assets of various sorts encourages people to make various kinds of investment. For example, the Commission on Social Justice recommends the introduction of a set of Individual Learning Accounts as part of an 'Investors'' future. These accounts would be dedicated to encouraging people to support throughout their working lives. These accounts would be made available to all after they have left compulsory education. The accounts would contain seed capital from government as well as money from the individuals themselves. People would use their accounts to purchase training modules supplied from a range of providers.

Assets focus on the stock of resources owned by an individual. This looks at things such as savings, pensions and home-ownership. This contrasts with the flow of resources going to an individual. Within social policy, flows are usually in the form of income payments. Although assets and income as stocks and flows are different entities, they can nevertheless be converted into one another. Income can be saved up to provide a stock of savings, and a house can be sold off to generate a flow of income to the individual. This raises a question about why one would prefer to distribute assets rather than income. If it is the underlying resource (money) rather than the form the resource takes (assets or income) that is important, then asset-based welfare does not provide a substantially different alternative to a traditional emphasis on income benefits. Michael Sherraden writes that an important objection to asset-based welfare holds that, 'Both flows and stocks (income and assets) are important, but nothing about inequality or poverty *turns* on the distinction ... Is a spring or a pond more valuable as a source of water? Water is clearly what is important. Likewise, *command over resources* is what is important regarding poverty and inequality' (Sherraden 1991, 145).

Asset effect

In reply to this supporters of asset-based welfare argue that asset-ownership has a distinctive impact an individual behaviour and welfare. In short, assets are associated with a distinctive 'asset-effect'. On this view, people are more likely to invest if they possess assets rather than income. Michael Sherraden first proposed the notion of an asset-effect (Paxton 2001). He says that, 'income only maintains consumption, but assets change the way people think and interact in the world. With assets, people begin to think in the long term and pursue long-term goals. In other words, while incomes feed people's stomachs, assets change their heads' (Sherraden 1991, 6). Sherraden (1991) argues that the asset effect can be broken down into nine main components. First, asset-ownership promotes household stability. He says that the ownership of assets provides people with a cushion against unfortunate events or shocks. For example, owning assets helps people cope with the loss of a job, by providing resources they can fall back on while looking for work. Second, assets create an orientation towards the future. The process of acquiring and accumulating assets encourages people to plan ahead and take a long-term view of their welfare. Third, assets support the development of human capital. Owning assets encourages people to learn how best to manage and invest their assets. Fourth, assets enable focus and specialisation. Sherraden argues that ever since

Adam Smith, economists have recognised the importance of specialisation for economic development. Smith pointed to the benefits
that arise from a division of labour. Sherraden says that assets stimu-
late people to focus on particular life-paths, and so encourages specialisation. Fifth, assets provide a base for risk-taking. With the
security furnished by the possession of assets, people are more likely
to undertake entrepreneurial activities (which necessarily have an
element of risk), and this entrepreneurial behaviour provides a basis
for innovation. Sixth, owning assets increases personal efficacy.
Assets allow for greater prediction and control, and so frees up time
for other endeavours. Seventh, assets increase social influence.
Owning an asset can enhance one's standing in the community,
and foster social capital in the form of networks of protection and
information sources. In addition, assets give people support in their
negotiations with others preventing them from being simply pushed
around or ignored. Eighth, assets support political participation. He
says that people with assets have greater incentives and resources to
take part in the political process to protect these assets. Ninth, asset-
ownership increases the welfare of children. He says that assets
provide, 'an intergenerational connection that income and consumption cannot provide' (Sherraden 1991, 166). Sherraden notes
that the transmission of assets from parent to child has important
intergenerational effects, and that the desire to leave assets for their
offspring provides an important motor for people to accumulate
assets.

Michael Sherraden recognises that some facets of the asset-effect
may be replicated by income-based policies. He notes that social
influence may come from consuming conspicuous or luxury items
(such as expensive cars). Alternatively, increasing income may
provide people with a greater incentive to participate in the political
process in order to protect their income (for example by voting for
parties that promise not to increase taxes). Although Sherraden
accepts that income can generate such effects, he says that assets
have at least two advantages over a putative 'income effect'. First,
the link between assets and its effects is more direct and substantial
than any effects tied to income. This arises because assets provide
people with a degree of control that is lacking with income. He suggests that while income payments do not leave much control to
individuals, assets place control firmly in their hands. This is impor-

tant because this individual control is more likely to lead to sort of effects to which he draws attention. Second, he argues that income and assets also offer different perspectives on the issue of the distribution of economic surplus. He suggests that income-based approaches concentrate on distributing resources from a fixed amount of surplus generated by the economy. The income approach does not look at how this surplus is produced. In contrast, the asset approach seeks to add to the surplus as well as share out resources: it focuses on production as well as distribution. He says that asset-based welfare does not focus on social development alone, but promotes economic and social development.

Evidence on the asset-effect

The notion of an asset-effect raises a series of issues. Perhaps the most obvious issue is whether or not an asset-effect actually exists. That is, does owning an asset cause people to think differently about the world? Even if an asset-effect is deemed to exist, other points need to be addressed. A second issue concerns the precise mechanics of any asset-effect. What aspect of asset-ownership is responsible for the asset-effect? Does the mere fact of holding an asset generate an asset-effect, or is the process of using or deploying assets (such as saving into an asset) primarily responsible for changing the way people think? A third issue is whether owning an asset is the best way of fostering the asset-effect. The effect associated with the ownership of assets might also emerge with other policies, and if this occurs the question arises as to whether or not holding an asset is the best way of producing the desired effect. For example, increased spending on primary education might be a more cost effective way of inculcating a saving habit among the young rather than providing children with an asset designed to encourage saving. The second and third issues build upon the first question. For example, it only makes sense to explore the underlying mechanics of an asset-effect if an asset-effect is presumed to exist.

It is difficult to make progress on these matters without resort to evidence. However, a key problem facing asset-based welfare is that the evidence on the effects of asset-ownership, though growing, is fairly small. Much of the literature has focused on the first and most immediate issue, namely whether or not an asset-effect actually exists. Currently, the body of evidence suggests the presence of an asset-effect, although this view is not unanimous. The controversial nature of the asset-effect means that less progress has been made on addressing the other points above. Michael Sherraden helped found a Center for Social Development at the University of Washington at Missouri, and an important part of the work of this Center involves conducting empirical studies on asset-ownership. Between 1997 and 2001, the Center for Social Development was home to the existence of the Individual Development Account initiative as part of a research project entitled the American Dream Demonstration. Mark Schreiner, Margaret Clancy and Michael Sherraden (2002) note that as of December 2001, there were 2,364 people participating in this study within thirteen host organisations across the United States. Fifty six per cent of enrollees were labelled 'savers', that is people who saved a net of $100 or more as of December 31 2001. Net deposits are defined as matchable deposits plus interest (net of fees) minus unmatched withdrawals. Forty four per cent of people are 'low savers', having saved up to a net of $100 as of December 31. The average participant made a deposit at half yearly intervals, and saved around $1 for every $2 that could be matched. The average monthly net deposit was $19.07. The average participant saved around $700 per year. The largest share of matched withdrawals was used for buying a home (28 per cent), starting a business (23 per cent), post secondary education (21 per cent) and home repair (18 per cent). Mark Schreiner, Margaret Clancy and Michael Sherraden argue that over half of the people in the IDA programme were savers and that a, 'noteworthy finding is that income is not related to being a saver, and has only small effects on the amount of savings' (Schreiner, Clancy, and Sherraden 2002, vii).

Gregory Mills, Rhiannon Patterson, Larry Orr and Donna DeMarco (2004) confirm these findings. As part of their investigation these researchers conducted a study at one of the sites that was part of the above project. These individuals examined whether IDAs promoted asset accumulation by tracking the behaviour of those who took part in the scheme as well as a control group that did not have access to these accounts. Of the 1,103 programme eligible participants who took part in this 4-year study, 537 people were randomly allocated to a treatment group and 566 people were put into a control group. The study found that the IDA programme had significant favourable effects on asset-building among low income individuals. The researchers found that those who participated in the IDA programme had significantly higher rates of home-ownership than treatment group members, and IDAs helped increase retirement savings and education achievement.

British studies provide a more mixed picture about the asset-effect. John Bynner (2001) reports research conducted by himself and Sofia Despotidou at the Institute of Education in London. Bynner says that it is important to track the behaviour of a particular set of people over time when exploring whether or not providing people with assets leads to a change in their behaviour or welfare. He states that longitudinal or panel data can provide an important source of such information. A panel data set tracks a given set or panel of individuals over time. For example, a specific set of individuals might take part in a study that requires them to complete a survey every year for a given period of time. In Britain, there are a number of ongoing panel studies. One of these datasets, the National Child Development Survey, provides some information relevant for those researching into an asset-effect. The National Child Development Survey is a dataset that tracks people born between March 3–9 1958. Surveys have been conducted at ages 7, 11, 16, 23 and 33. Approximately, 12,000 people from an original set of 16,500 individuals are still participating today. In the survey at age 23, individuals were asked questions relating savings, investments and inheritance.

Drawing on Michael Sherraden's work, Bynner and Despotidou sought to examine whether there were any links between asset-ownership at 23 and subsequent welfare outcomes at 33. They split welfare outcomes into a number of components. They looked in particular at economic outcomes (such as years spent in full-time education, and years spent in unemployment), health (such as degree of mental illness, whether or not a person smokes, and an individual's general health), citizenship and values (whether an individual voted in the last election, political interest and work ethic) and parenting outcomes (for example, how often parents read to children).

Bynner and Despotidou adopt a three-stage procedure to test for the effects of assets on these different welfare outcomes. First, the impact of different assets (in particular, savings, investment and inheritance) was analysed separately. Controlling for factors such as social class and education, it was found that savings had the strongest connection to outcomes, with investments having a much weaker link and inheritance having hardly any effect. In the second stage, inheritance was dropped from the analysis, and the combined effect of savings and investment, savings or investment, and neither savings or investment were investigated. It was found that little was gained by combining savings and investment in this fashion, and so in the third step the effects of savings and investment were analysed separately.

Bynner and Despotidou found that the data supported the idea of an asset-effect. They discovered that positive experience within the workforce appeared to be strongly dependent on assets, especially in relation to employment history. With respect to health, it was found that people possessing assets at 23 were less likely to smoke at 33, and savings at 33 were linked to subsequent good physical and mental health. As regards citizenship and values, political interest is positively linked to owning assets, as are trust in the political system and a commitment to a work ethic. However, assets did not display a link to voting behaviour, and there was not strong evidence of positive effects on parenting. Bynner and Despotidou note that only modest amounts of assets were needed to generate the effects observed.

Bynner's and Despotidou's study has been influential in policy debates in Britain. David Blunkett (2001), the former Labour Secretary of State for Education, highlights this study in his case for asset-based welfare in his book *Politics and Progress*. Similarly, Her Majesty's Treasury (2001a) cites this evidence in its analysis of asset-based welfare. Although Bynner's and Despotidou's work is influential, their work is not unchallenged. Carl Emmerson and Matthew Wakefield (2001) question the interpretation and nature of their findings. Emmerson and Wakefield note that this study found that savings were linked with subsequent good outcomes, but say that a high proportion of 23 year olds in this research (82 percent) reported having savings at 23. Emmerson and Wakefield argue that this large proportion does not distinguish between those who were active savers and those who simply had modest amounts left over in their current account. Emmerson and Wakefield say that these are two categories of individuals, and grouping them together as savers masks important differences between these active and passive savers. To avoid this, Emmerson and Wakefield prefer to say that lack of savings seem to be associated with the greater likelihood of bad outcomes, rather than saving is linked with good outcomes. Beyond this issue of interpretation, Emmerson and Wakefield raise several questions about the nature of the results. First, they ask whether savings genuinely cause good outcomes or whether the association of savings and beneficial outcomes is coincidental. They say it may be possible that the link between savings and outcomes is in fact explained by some other variable, and suggest that the ability to plan ahead might be a candidate for such a variable. Second, they say that even if it can be shown that savings do cause outcomes, the precise mechanics behind this 'asset-effect' is unclear. Is it holding savings that makes the difference, or is it the process of saving that is important? They state that the precise way the asset-effect oper-ates is important for developing policy recommendations. Emmerson and Wakefield argue that the fact that inheritances do not appear to have an asset-effect may suggest that it is not holding an asset that makes a difference. Third, Emmerson and Wakefield say that Bynner's and Despotidou's findings only relate to one point in time (at age 33). Emmerson and Wakefield continue that any causal link between savings and outcomes may change over time as other variables (such as university education) come into play.

Stephen McKay and Elaine Kempson (2003) question the ex-istence of an asset-effect in work done for the Department of Work and Pensions in England on savings and life events. McKay and Kempson base their analysis on the British Household Panel Survey (BHPS) for 1991–2000. The BHPS is an annual panel data survey of 5,000 households. McKay and Kempson explore two things relating to the asset-effect. First, they examine whether savings has an effect on outcomes. McKay and Kempson looked at those individuals who were 55 or younger in 1995 who also took part in the wave of the BHPS in 2000. These researchers say that this part of the study repli-cates the findings of Bynner and Despotidou, namely that assets appear to be linked with positive health and labour market out-comes. For example, those with savings were less likely to smoke (non-smoking being an important measure of good health). McKay and Kempson continue that the effects may be more important for men than women. Second, they explore whether assets were linked to changes in behaviour between 1995 and 2000 as opposed to positive outcomes at 2000. McKay and Kempson argue that studying changes in behaviour represents a superior way of analysing the asset-effect rather than concentrating on outcomes alone. They say that asset-ownership is much more weakly associated (if at all) with changes in behaviour between 1995 and 2000. They write that they found, 'no reliable effects on life outcomes' (McKay and Kempson, 2003).

The incentives approach

An alternative rationale for assets is grounded in an incentives approach. Unlike models of the asset-effect, this line of thought does not suggest that the possession of assets stimulates the development of individual character. Rather, the provision of assets alters the incentives faced by individuals in such a way that enhances economic efficiency. People's character may remain the same, only now people have more incentive to select one course of action over another.

Samuel Bowles and Herbert Gintis (1998) provide an example of this approach. They highlight the, 'inefficient incentive structures that arise in economies with highly unequal asset distributions' (Bowles and Gintis 1998, 7). Bowles and Gintis have an overarching commitment to equality. They say that the attachment to equality is a defining feature of progressive politics. They continue that strategies to promote equality are more likely to succeed where it can be shown that equality boosts efficiency. For example, this can help defeat the objection that while equality might be a laudable aim, it ought to be resisted because of the losses it imposes on the efficiency of an economy.

Bowles and Gintis say that equality in the distribution of assets provides an example of the way that equality can enhance efficiency. Samuel Bowles and Herbert Gintis deploy mainstream economic theory to advance a case for distributing assets. In particular, they draw on principal-agent analysis. Principal-agent theory refers to situations in which one individual or set of individuals – the principal – instructs another individual or set of individuals – the agent – to make decisions on their behalf. For example, the owner of a company may employ a board of managers to make the daily decisions about the running of the company. This devolution of decision-making creates the possibility of conflict between principals and agents. In particular, principals and agents will each have their own interests, and these interests may conflict rather than coincide. For example, the owners of a corporation may wish the company to maximise profits, while managers might prefer instead to maximise the size of the firm, even though this may reduce profits. This conflict gives rise to an 'agency problem', namely, how can principals ensure that agents act on their behalf.

One obvious solution is for principals to write a contract that guarantees that agents pursue the principal's interests. For example, company owners could write a contract that requires managers to maximise company profits. Although complete contracts can in principle resolve the agency problem, lack of information undermines the principal's capacity to write a comprehensive set of contracts. It is usually impossible to predict all the situations that might arise in the future, and this means that a principal cannot plan for every eventuality in a contract. Bowles and Gintis argue that the conflict of interests plus incomplete information leads to economic inefficiency. In the absence of complete contracts, principals are drawn into monitoring the actions of agents in order to alleviate the agency problem. This monitoring implies costs and does not guarantee that the agency problem will be resolved. This is inefficient because these costs would not arise if it were possible to write a comprehensive set of contracts.

Bowles and Gintis suggest that the heart of the agency problem is the fact that those making decisions, the agents, do not bear the full consequences of their actions. Their solution is to ensure agents bear these consequences. They say that to do this productive assets should be transferred from principals to agents. Schemes to spread employee share-ownership and tenant home-ownership are presented as examples of this approach. Bowles and Gintis state that the productivity of firms depends crucially upon the efforts of employees. They say that while employers want workers to work hard, employees may wish to take things at a more leisurely pace. The employers (principal) and employees (agent) desire different levels of effort. One way to resolve this is for employers to specify levels of effort in a contract. However, workers are better informed than employers over the level of effort they exert. This privileged information means that contracts cannot resolve this agency problem. Bowles and Gintis argue that if productive assets were placed in the hands of employees, then the incentives would change so that the interests of employers and employees are aligned. If employees were presented with shares in the company, then their efforts would impinge directly on the returns they enjoy. Low efforts would deflate the value of their share, while high efforts would increase the value of their financial asset. Ownership stakes provide employees with a material incentive to work hard.

Bowles and Gintis argue that in the housing rental market, landlords delegate the daily upkeep of their properties to their tenants. While landlords may wish tenants to spend considerable time and effort in ensuring the property is well looked after, tenants may prefer to spend their time doing other things. While landlords could try and specify level of care in a rental contract, the fact that tenants are better informed than landlords about the level of care they exert means that any contract will not be comprehensive. Landlords will incur costs in monitoring tenant behaviour, for example the time and resources involved in making regular checks of the condition of the property. Bowles and Gintis say that these monitoring costs could be avoided if ownership stakes are distributed to tenants. If tenants have ownership stakes, then they are directly affected by the decisions they make. Tenants will benefit if they take good care of their stake (for example, by increasing the value of their home)

Bowles and Gintis acknowledge that a natural question provoked by their analysis is that if transferring assets from principals to agents does indeed lead to efficiency gains, then why do we not see more of these asset distributions within the economy. For example, if worker owned firms enhance efficiency, then why are such firms in a minority within most countries? Bowles and Gintis contend that structural factors impede the transfer of assets from principals to agents. For instance, employees are constrained from borrowing from banks which would allow them to purchase stakes for precisely the reason that employee share-ownership is intended to overcome. In particular, financial institutions are reluctant to lend to workers because employees are better informed about the level of effort they will undertake to pay back the loan.

Matching

One popular way of providing people with incentives is to have a matching element to an asset policy. Matching involves some public or private agency providing a match for a contribution made by an asset-holder. For example, a matched savings scheme might involve the state providing a financial match for savings made by an individual person. The match can be less than, equal or more than the contribution made by a person, and the particular rate offered may differ for different people (for example, more generous matches may be made available for lower-income individuals). An upper limit might also be set on the total funds that a person may be able to attract.

Superficially, matches can provide individuals with powerful incentives to accumulate savings. A matched contribution may exceed the returns that a person receives from using their money elsewhere, and this provides individuals with an incentive to save in to an asset. Although matching appears to provide people with good incentives to save or invest, there may be a number of problems with this sort of scheme. In the introduction to this chapter it was noted that designing incentive schemes may not be easy. One potential problem with matching concerns whether this provokes genuinely new saving. People might already have been intending to save, and matching here does not provoke any additional saving. Matching now constitutes a 'deadweight' cost. Alternatively, a matching scheme may encourage 'borrowing to save', whereby people borrow sums on money (on credit cards say) to get funds that will trigger off matching payments. People use loans to exploit the funds available for matching (Emmerson and Wakefield 2003). That a simple mechanism such as matching can potentially give rise to such effects highlights that it may not be easy to design incentive schemes within assets.

Evidence is important for deciding whether matching does in fact provide people to conduct genuinely new savings. As with the asset-effect, the data on this matter is modest. However, evidence exists which suggests that matching can provide incentives to save. In Britain, a matched savings scheme, the Savings Gateway, was piloted between August 2002 and November 2004. This was held at five locations across England. Participants in the pilots were drawn from families in which household income is £11,000 or less, or £15,000 or less from those households with dependant children. Elaine Kempson, Stephen McKay and Sharon Collard (2005) in an evaluation of this pilot estimate that if these qualifying conditions are rolled out nationally, then between 25 and 34 per cent of the working age population would be able to open a Saving Gateway. The pilot involved around 1,500 participants, with roughly 1,000 people being provided with a Saving Gateway and 500 people who didn't have a Saving Gateway being assigned to a control group. Under the pilot scheme, people can save up to £25 per month, which builds to a maximum of £375. Once the account matures at 18 months, the government adds a matching contribution of £1 for every £1 saved for the highest balance achieved during the lifetime of the account.

Kempson, Stephen McKay and Sharon Collard found evidence of a link between assets and savings behaviour. Kempson, McKay and Collard note that of those taking part in the Saving Gateway pilot, just over half already had a savings account. However, less than two in ten of participants had savings of £500 or more. The researchers found that the average amount saved in the Saving Gateway was £282, with about half saving the maximum £375. While 17 per cent of participants said they had been saving regularly before the account, 39 per cent of people said they saved regularly by standing order or direct debit and an additional 38 per cent said they put money regularly by cash or cheque. The average monthly deposit was £16.14, with the most common deposits each month being the maximum £25 or nothing. Interviews revealed that two thirds of participants aimed to continue to save at the end of the pilot (most had not been regular savers before). The researchers found that three months after the accounts matured, over 90 per cent of Saving Gateway participants had a savings account of some kind and approximately 40 per cent were still saving fairly regularly. Kempson, McKay and Collard conclude that the Saving Gateway seems to have attracted genuinely new saving by encouraging people to start saving or increase the amounts they were already saving.

Ruth Lister argues that the results of the Saving Gateway pilot suggests that this policy could help people cope with poverty. She argues that those in poverty deploy a range of strategies to 'get by' each month. This includes getting into debt to help cope with their fluctuations in income and spending needs. Lister says that the Saving Gateway results suggests that savings could assist people because this appears to enhance their sense of financial security, and to a lesser extent, give them greater control over their own lives. However, Lister cautions against using savings alone as a way of tackling poverty, and insists that the Saving Gateway should exist alongside increased spending on income benefits and better access to more affordable credit (Lister and Sodha 2006).

Hybrid approaches

Although the character development and incentives models represent different ways of thinking about assets within social policy, elements of these different wings can be combined to form a hybrid approach. Frank Field (1996; 2000) combines elements of both character development and incentives in his analysis of stakeholder welfare and stakeholder pensions. Field's overriding concern is to promote character development within welfare policy. He is concerned that the welfare state encourages the sort of dependency culture described by Julian Le Grand and David Nissan. Although Field wishes to foster character development, he says that any approach must be grounded in a realistic theory of human motivations. People must be willing to develop appropriate virtues. Field continues that any realistic theory must acknowledge the core role played by self-interest. This emphasis on self-interest means that attention should be paid to the incentives that people have to develop their character. He notes that, 'No welfare system can function effectively if it is not based on a realistic view of human nature. Self-interest, not altruism is mankind's main driving force' (Field 1996, 19). Field continues that once a person's character has developed it may be possible to reduce the part played by self-interest in developing character. While it might be possible to downplay incentives in the long run, in the early stages of policy, attention should be placed on how incentives can help foster individual character. Field says that individual ownership chimes with incentives because it provides a means through which individuals can capture directly the benefits of their own actions.

Differences between character development and incentives approach

The character development and incentives approaches point to different models of assets. This section considers some of the overlaps and differences that exist within asset-based welfare. I concentrate on the availability of assets; the temporal dimension to assets; restrictions on use; and education.

Availability

Availability considers the extent to which assets are made available throughout the population. The character development school of thought is compatible with both universal and targeted schemes. One view is that opportunities for the development of character abound throughout any person's life, and so assets should be made available to all. An alternative view is that certain groups of people may encounter particular difficulties in developing and so targeted assistance should be provided for these individuals. For example, low-income individuals may face difficulties in saving, and so asset-policies may be aimed at helping these people to save.

The incentives framework is also compatible with both universal or targeted measures. The incentives approach assumes that people respond to incentives. As the ownership of assets is thought to be a way of providing people with incentives to behave in particular ways, then fostering incentives suggests it is valuable to encourage ownership for all. A matched savings account that provides contributions from public and private agencies could provide everyone with incentives to make savings. While the incentives approach can support universal policies, Samuel Bowles' and Herbert Gintis' principal-agent perspective generates a more selective approach. Bowles and Gintis note that principals not agents own assets. Their aim is to provide assets to agents. By focusing attention on agents, the Bowles and Gintis model points to a targeted approach. The emphasis on agents can nonetheless have a wide coverage. For example, company employees are likely to constitute a significant part of the population. If substantial numbers do not own company shares, then a scheme to spread employee share-ownership involves large numbers.

Although the character development and incentives approaches are both compatible with universal and targeted schemes, progressive models express a bias towards universal policies. Reformists often call for the implementation of an 'inclusive' asset policy (Kelly and Lissauer 2000; Sherraden 2003; White 2006). Michael Sherraden says that the, 'goal should be an asset-based policy that is large scale and fully inclusive, with progressive funding, so that everyone participates and has resources for life investments and social protections' (Sherraden 2003, 33). Michael Sherraden argues that one of the problems facing current asset policies is that they are regressive, that is they favour those individuals that already own assets. He says that an inclusive approach should extend beyond these boundaries and enable all to possess assets. By stressing ownership for all, inclusion exhibits a bias towards universal initiatives. Although universal schemes are important for progressive approaches, they also appear in conservative models. For example, the British Conservative party's Lifetime Savings Account is an initiative that is open to all. The main difference between progressive and conservative models relates to the means used to implement a universal scheme. Reformists are more likely than conservatives to endorse the redistribution of property. Creating an inclusive approach is likely to involve a redistribution of current patterns of asset-ownership, transferring resources from the asset rich to the asset poor. While conservative accounts may favour universal schemes, they tend to eschew action by the state to guarantee ownership for all.

A separate but related issue concerns whether participation in an asset scheme is made compulsory or voluntary. Paul Marshall (2004) sets out a compulsory scheme that requires everyone to open and save into a personal pensions account to supplement the pension they receive from the state. In contrast, Michael Sherraden's model of Individual Development Accounts is a voluntary scheme. Sherraden argues that asset initiatives should fall within a framework of liberty, and liberty dictates that individuals should be allowed to accept or reject an asset (although as we shall see he nevertheless supports placing restrictions on how assets are used and it is arguable whether the commitment to voluntary assets and restrictions is consistent). Generally speaking, character development models can be used to support compulsory or voluntary approaches. Although Sherraden suggests that people should be free to reject character development, the commitment to ensure that people develop could be used to justify a policy of compelling people to participate in an asset scheme. The incentives standpoint tends to favour voluntary rather than compulsory initiatives. If an asset is sufficiently attractive to individuals, then there is no need to compel people to take up assets. People will simply take up assets of their own accord.

Time

Time is important for assets in two main senses. First, the point at which the asset is first supplied to an individual. It could be provided to a person at birth, when they reach the age of majority, or the age at which they begin their working lives. Second, the life-span of the asset. Assets can have varying lifespans, such as 18 years for the Child Trust Fund or a working lifetime for a Lifetime Savings Account.

For the character development approach, assets should be provided to people at the point at which development should begin. This is likely to vary depending upon the particular social policy goal in question. For example, if the aim is to use an asset to help young children to develop a savings habit, then the asset should be provided before they start school. Alternatively, if the objective is to ensure that people make investments once they have left school, then the asset could be provided at the point at which they leave compulsory education. The character development approach thus allows a range of starting points, and these starting points can occur before, during or after they are regarded as adult citizens. Character development must occur over a period of time. Development requires that people have the time to change. Holding an asset is thought to be important for initiating and supporting change during the process of development. The lifespan of assets depends on the period of development in question, and different periods of development mean that different assets have different lifespans. For example, the Child Trust Fund is 18 years to help support a savings habit and knowledge of financial matters from birth until young adulthood. In contrast, the Individual Development Account model piloted by the Center for Social Development lasted for 4 years.

On the incentives view, the provision of an asset should be made at the point at which people are able to respond to incentives. Generally speaking, this is unlikely to cover young children. On the Bowles and Gintis approach, assets should be provided at the point at which people find themselves in principal-agent situations. Typically, this occurs after they have left school, for instance when they start working for a company or renting a home. This aspect of timing introduces one difference between the character development and incentive approaches over the nature of assets. The character development approach allows for the provision of assets before they reach the stage of entering these principal-agent relationships. Thus, they allow assets to be provided before they are relevant for an incentives mode of thinking. Once individuals have become economic agents, they will respond continually to incentives. Consequently, they should be allowed to hold assets as long as these incentives are relevant. For employees, they should own shares at least throughout their working lives.

Restrictions on use

The character development approach is compatible with policies that impose restrictions on how assets are used, as well as measures that allow people to use assets as they please. In the United States, Individual Development Accounts are supposed to be used for starting a business, putting a deposit on a home or funding investments in post-compulsory education. In Britain, Conservative party proposals for a Lifetime Savings Account are suppose to be used for funding investments in post-compulsory education. Pragmatic arguments can be used to support a case for or against restrictions. Restrictions might be thought to be a useful tool for guiding people to develop in particular ways. Specifying that people can only spend funds on starting a business, buying a home or investing in skills, might help encourage people to be forward-looking about their personal development and take the steps needed to guarantee their security in the future. On this view, restrictions could help educate or teach people about their personal development. A different view might hold that although restrictions could in principle aid a person's character development, difficulties are likely to be encountered when trying to put this into practice. People may be able to get around restrictions and public and private agencies may be reluctant to come forward to monitor any restrictions. The balance of such pragmatic considerations could help decide whether or not restrictions are imposed for the asset in question.

The incentives approach suggests that restrictions on use are unnecessary or go beyond the incentives framework. The incentives approach concentrates on providing people with incentives to pursue particular courses of action, for example starting a business, buying a home or paying for training. If people have sufficient incentives to use their assets for such investments, then specifying that assets can only be used for these purposes is redundant. Establishing and monitoring restrictions is a costly exercise and so outlining restrictions imposes an unnecessary financial burden. If it is difficult to provide people with incentives to pursue a particular path or paths, then the desirability of these options ought to be questioned. Implementing restrictions in this case implies going beyond the boundaries of the incentives approach.

Education

Education provides an example of the different policies used to support asset initiatives in a character development and incentives approach. Character development models usually combine assets with a programme of education. Michael Sherraden (1991) says that, 'Asset accounts could be used as a basis for economic education and planning for the future' (Sherraden 1991, 204). Character development is often thought to involve an element of learning. Education is thought to help people change or develop. While learning can involve the practical knowledge or 'learning by doing' gained from the experience of holding an asset, character development approaches often suggest an element of formal instruction is important for fostering development. In the United States, holders of Individual Development Accounts are required to attend educational classes as a condition of their participation in this initiative. In Britain, the Labour government has stated that it intends that holders of the Child Trust Fund will receive lessons at school on how to manage their Child Trust Fund. In contrast, education is not needed in the incentives approach. As no attempt is made to change or mould individual preferences, incentive models tend to restrict themselves to the provision of information to individuals rather than use education to encourage change.

Funding

Asset-based welfare will involve the commitment of substantial financial resources. Money will be required for both the initial provision of assets as well as during the lifetime of the asset. Michael Sherraden highlights the importance of cost for the character development approach when he comments that the, 'biggest policy issue is cost. To what extent would asset-based welfare be paid for out of the cost of existing programs, and to what extent would new money be required' (Sherraden 1991, 227). Sherraden (1991) estimates that the cost to the federal government for the first year of providing Individual Development Account programmes for education, housing, self-employment and retirement would be $28.6 billion. The cost of each of the programmes consists of the initial funding going into the Individual Development Account as well as the tax breaks that the account would attract. For example, Sherraden says that for housing Individual Development Accounts, if the federal government made up three quarters of the average annual deposit of $1,500 for the five million households who fall below the poverty line, then this seed capital would cost the federal government $5.6 billion. He continues that the cost to the federal government of providing tax breaks into these accounts for the poor would cost $1.2 billion, while tax incentives for the non-poor would cost $4.9 billion. Thus the total cost to the federal government of providing housing Individual Development Accounts for the first year of the programme (adding the seed capital and tax breaks) amounts to $11.7 billion. The Bowles and Gintis model of incentives concentrates on redistributing assets from principals to agents and so does not appear to have the same financial implications as the character development. However, incentives models that have a matched savings element imply significant cost implications to guarantee the matched contributions element.

Taxes are an obvious way of paying for assets. Many proposals on paying for assets focus on the role played by wealth taxes. I shall explore the different types of wealth tax in more depth in the next chapter. This is because wealth taxes tend to play a more prominent role in models of assets within the realm of citizenship. Although wealth taxes are a feature of social policy proposals, social policy models are more open to using a range of taxes to pay for assets. For example, Michael Sherraden (1991) suggests that taxes placed on existing income related social security benefits in the United States could be used to pay for Individual Development Accounts.

Instead of raising taxes, government could alternatively make cuts from other spending programmes to fund asset policies. Michael Sherraden (1991) argues although it may be tempting to call for new taxes to help pay for asset-based initiatives, it is more realistic politically to look for how asset policies could be funded by diverting money from current government programmes elsewhere. He says that legislators are usually reluctant to make calls for new money, and this reluctance intensifies where there are budget deficits in government spending. Sherraden continues that although cuts in defence spending are often touted as ways of funding social policy programme, it may be wiser to see how any saving cuts might be generated from within social security budgets (Sherraden 1991).

Michael Sherraden advances a plausible set of arguments about public spending. It is probably easier to persuade legislators to reallocate existing expenditures rather than raise new money. In reallocating government spending, it is also probably easier to shift money within rather than between particular policy areas. Each policy area is associated with a specific set of interests, ranging from the politician at the head of the relevant department, the civil servants who implement departmental policies and the individuals and groups who benefit from these policies. Trying to transfer money across areas, from agriculture to social security say, is often likely to encounter more resistance among interested parties rather than reallocating money within a particular policy area. Added to this general problem of moving money between policy areas are problems associated specifically with the proposal to cut spending from defence. Writing in 1991, Sherraden acknowledges that some savings might be available in defence spending as a result of a 'peace dividend' following the end of the Cold War. In the early 21st century, however, it is unlikely that current commitments to address issues such as terrorism mean the continued existence of a peace dividend. Furthermore, unpopular areas of spending such as defence will probably receive widespread calls for savings, and it is unlikely that these competing demands will put proposals for asset-based welfare on a secure financial footing. Thus, when exploring how cuts in existing government programmes can be used to fund asset policies, it is probably safer to look at spending within the broad area of social services.

Writing in 1991, Michael Sherraden makes a number of suggestions of where resources might be diverted from the social security budget in the United States to help pay for a programme of Individual Development Accounts. Many of his proposals involve reducing government subsidies for what he considers to be regressive asset-related policies. For instance, he advocates reducing tax relief on interest payments for mortgages on second homes or for homes whose value is above the price of a median house. Sherraden argues that subsidies on these luxury items would be better spent on providing ownership for all.

Much of Sherraden's focus is on reallocating money from asset-related policies. On a broader level, efforts might be made to divert money from other areas within the social security level. Non-asset related areas of spending fall mainly into one of two main camps. First, spending on income-related benefits. This covers income payments to help people cope with things such as sickness, unemployment, housing and education (such as schools or universities) and health (such as hospitals or nursing homes). Money for assets could come from cuts in income payments, public services or some combination of income payments and public services. For example, reductions in child related income benefits could be used to help provide capital grants for children at birth. Cuts in government spending for universities could be used to help fund Individual Development Accounts. The issue of what other areas of welfare spending could be cut for assets touches on a broader question of the appropriate relationship of asset-based welfare to other arms of welfare policy. I shall return to this issue below.

Other agencies

Asset-based social theory does not suggest that the state should be the only funder of assets. A range of other agencies from both the public and private sectors, such as local councils and private companies, could help pay for assets. These other agencies could have an important role for assets for a variety of reasons. One objective of asset-based welfare may be to assist on the development of 'social capital' that is the network of ties that link different people within society. One way of enhancing such ties is to encourage the links that people have with collective organisations within civil society. Funding arrangements might help bolster these connections. A matched scheme might be put in operation that means that individual savings into an asset scheme attract a matching contribution from an organisation. Organisations will probably only invest in assets if they gain some benefits from investment. Thus, funding arrangements are likely to be more successful if they tie into the goals of an organisation. Community development bodies might be attracted to invest in schemes that aim to help people start their own business, private companies might match funds placed for certain types of investment in education and training.

Other bodies might also be important for relieving budget constraints on the state. The state might find it difficult to generate spending on assets from additional taxes or reallocating existing public spending commitments. Other organisations could be involved in helping raise the extra funds needed for assets. For example Dominic Maxwell and Sonia Sodha (2006) suggest that other agencies could be involved in making payments into the Child Trust Funds for children from less privileged backgrounds. They note that certain children (such as those in local authority care) may not find it easy to save into their Child Trust Funds. They say that this could be a source of inequality as children from more privileged backgrounds may be better able to save into their Child Trust Fund accounts, thereby accumulating a larger Child Trust Fund. They say that to stem this inequality, policy should explore how additional contributions might be placed into the accounts for these children. They say that while the state could be involved in making such contributions, the size of the additional contributions would probably exceed the government's constraints on spending. Maxwell and Sodha argue that public policy should examine how other agencies could be encouraged to make contributions into the funds owned by these less privileged children.

Relationship of assets to income and public services

So far I have discussed two key strands of thought feeding into asset-based welfare. I now discuss the relationship of assets to other forms of welfare policy. Asset-based welfare is only one type of welfare policy. The two main other sorts of welfare intervention are policies that provide people with income benefits as well as public services such as health and education. These other types of welfare intervention have already been mentioned in a number of contexts. For example, Michael Sherraden introduces asset-based ideas by contrasting it with conventional redistribution of income conducted by the state. Sherraden also notes in his discussion of how asset policies could be funded that money could come from cuts in spending on public services elsewhere.

The existence of these other forms of welfare policy raises the issue of what is the appropriate relationship of asset and non-asset policies. What is the proper mix of income and asset policies, and how should assets relate to public services? It is possible to imagine a range of scenarios. Assets might be seen as a substitute for both income benefits and public services and the welfare system as a whole would concentrate on providing people with a host of assets and minimise the provision of income benefits and public services. Alternatively, both income benefits and public services could be viewed as substantial aspects of policy and assets as a complement rather than substitute for these other sorts of policy.

Both the character development and incentives school of thought suggest that there should be a role for income policies and public services alongside assets. The character development approach presents asset-based welfare as an example of 'preventative' welfare. Other policies are important both for ensuring the success of prevention as well as addressing the limits of prevention. We have seen above that education features in models of individual development. Education presumes the existence of education services. For example, the Child Trust Fund focuses on lessons provided at school. Education for assets is not confined to school level education. The Individual Development Account initiative has a role for post-compulsory education. These lessons could be provided at the workplace or in colleges. If restrictions are imposed on the use of assets, then institutions will be needed to establish and monitor restrictions. Income is important because individuals will probably also find it easier to invest if their immediate consumption needs are met (such as food and clothing), and this highlights the significance of income benefits to guarantee a specified standard of living.

Income policies and public services are important for the continuing need for curative policies. While prevention may be preferable to cure as a general strategy, there are circumstances in which cure in unavoidable. Some people may be incapable of making investments, such as certain categories of the mentally ill and long-term sick. Also, people may be subject to 'shocks' during their life, for example the sudden loss of a job, and while assets can help cushion the blow, it is likely that other forms of welfare policy will be important. Public services can help with issues of long-term dependency such as chronic illness while income benefits can help people cope with unemployment.

Other types of policy are also likely to be important if investments fail. A person may be subject to a form of bad brute luck in their investments. For example, a person who invests part of their

Individual Development Account for training may lose their investment because their training organisation has committed a fraud by offering a bogus course. In this situation, income and public services could provide help for the effects of luck that a person has not entered voluntarily. Alternatively, people might be aware of various risks when they make investments. For this type of luck, namely the sort that people enter into voluntarily, there is a case for people to take some responsibility for their losses. Indeed, allowing losses may be considered part of the process of education. For example, helping people learn how to deal with the risks and returns in financial matters may involve permitting people to make losses in their financial investments. This is not inconsistent with an emphasis on placing restrictions on the use of assets. For example, a character development approach might endorse a restriction on how an asset is used to guide a particular form of development but within that restriction allow people to make mistakes as part of the process of character building.

One viewpoint rejects applying a principle of responsibility here, arguing that it is irrelevant whether a person experiences bad brute luck or voluntary 'option' luck when deciding whether to offer a person compensation. This perspective continues that equality demands that compensation be supplied whatever type of luck explains the loss (Anderson 1999). Alexander Kaufman (2004) notes, however, that if people suffer losses so severe that they fall below a prescribed minimum standard of living then there is a case for intervention whatever the type of luck. He continues that if losses do not push people below this standard of living, then there is a case for allowing people to take responsibility for their losses. This limits, but does not reject, the application of a principle of responsibility.

On the incentives approach, other types of policy will help sustain incentives as well as address the limitations of incentives. Schemes that use matching contributions to give people an incentive to save require income to provide the matching contributions. While a significant part of this income could come from the private sector, the public sector will probably also play an important role. The state is also likely to have to be involved in undertaking actions that redistribute property from principals to agents. Certain groups of people may also not be in a position to respond to incentives (such as the very young and mentally ill), and income benefits and public services will be important for these people.

Most proponents of asset-based welfare acknowledge the importance of income and public services. Michael Sherraden says that, 'Clearly, income-based policies will always play a role in welfare in the United States, probably the principal role. But this does not preclude the introduction of asset policies as complements where they are appropriate. The two basic types of policies – income-based and asset-based – can work together' (Sherraden 1991, 215–216). Similarly, in Britain the Labour party's 2001 general election manifesto declares that asset-based welfare forms a new pillar of welfare policy alongside the continuing focus on public services and income benefits (Labour party 2001). Although there is a belief that assets should exist alongside income and public services, the precise mix between these different strands of welfare can nevertheless be shaped in different ways. For example, the overall welfare mix might be skewed towards one type of policy, or alternatively all the strands might command equal emphasis. The balance between these different strands should perhaps ideally be shaped by the nature of the particular welfare problem in hand. Different policy issues could give rise to different mixes of asset, income and public services depending, for example, on the contribution that preventative and curative measures can play in overcoming the policy problem in question.

One concern with implementing asset-based policies might be that while governments may in theory be committed to seeing assets as a complement to income and public services, in practice administering assets would lead to the scaling back of other welfare policies. For example, budget constraints mean that pressures would be generated to cut either or both of public services or income benefits. Thus, if young people receive a Child Trust Fund that matures at 18, then government would use this as an opportunity to save money by cutting spending on higher education. Those young people who go on to university would be expected to pay a larger share of the cost of providing higher education out of their newly matured Child Trust Funds. Although this possibility ought to be acknowledged, at least two things can be said in reply to this concern. First, the problem of one type of policy 'crowding out' another is a general one and is not confined to assets. For example, increased levels of statutory maternity pay might create pressures to cut government spending on pre-school nurseries. As the problem of crowding out is a general one, it is challenge that cannot be avoided by shunning asset-based welfare. Second, although crowding out is a potential problem, there is nothing inevitable about increasing assets leading to cuts in other welfare policy. The challenge then is to create and maintain a political constituency that supports assets while continuing to back income benefits and public services. This is not necessarily a doomed project and so implementing assets does not inevitably imply the hollowing out of the rest of the welfare state.

Conclusion

This chapter has examined the assets agenda within the social policy arena. I have distinguished between two currents in social policy thinking, namely a 'character development' approach and an incentives framework. Although both strands believe that owning assets fosters a beneficial change in individual behaviour, the character development framework says that this behavioural change comes about by people developing character, while the incentives perspective suggests that owning assets alters the incentives faced by individuals.

This chapter has highlighted various issues for the character development and incentives wings of asset-based welfare. The 'asset-effect' is key to the character development stream of thought. Although evidence exists in the United States and Britain which backs the existence of an asset-effect, this evidence has been challenged. While evidence on the asset-effect is growing, it remains modest. Consequently, further work is needed on the asset-effect. Building on this is a second issue, namely, if an asset-effect is deemed to exist, then what are the channels through which an asset-effect operates. This second issue presumes the presence of an asset-effect and so cannot proceed properly until the first issue is addressed satisfactorily. The incentives view of assets raises the question of the extent of the incentives offered by asset-ownership. For example, how much genuinely new savings is generated by matched savings? A different issue for both strands concerns the appropriate relationship of asset-based welfare to income benefits and public services. Although asset-based welfare is an interesting development, questions remain about this agenda within social policy. Having considered asset-based welfare, the book proceeds now in the next chapter to examine the assets agenda within the realm of citizenship.

3
Citizenship

Introduction

This chapter considers the assets agenda within the realm of citizenship. The previous chapter looked at arguments about owning assets within the social policy field. Although 'asset-based welfare' shapes much of the way that assets are discussed today, Chapter 1 indicated that there is an alternative tradition feeding into this assets agenda. This has its origins in the work of individuals such as Thomas Paine and views the ownership of assets as an important element of citizenship. Thus, this chapter completes the exploration of the principal set of ideas informing the assets agenda that was started in Chapter 2.

As with social policy, the citizenship wing of the assets agenda is home to different approaches. Historically, two main traditions have shaped thinking about citizenship. First, the liberal approach views citizenship as a status that bestows a set of rights upon all members of a political community. In the period after the end of the Second World War this found classic expression in T.H. Marshall's (1950) *Citizenship and Social Class*. Marshall presents the modern version of citizenship in Britain as the steady accumulation since the 17th century of civil rights (such as freedom of expression), political rights (for example, the right to vote) and social rights (these cover rights of access to health and education services). Second, a more long-standing civic republican tradition that hails back to ancient Greece and Italy and adds to a set of rights various duties to act within the political community. These liberal and civic republican streams of thought define much of contemporary thinking about citizenship (Lister 1997; Miller 2000), although there have been recent attempts to outline versions of citizenship that go beyond the liberal and civic republican approaches, such as feminist citizenship and ecological citizenship (Lister 1997; Dobson 2004).

The liberal and civic republican traditions shape different versions of the assets agenda. A liberal approach presents the ownership of assets as part of the rights that should be enjoyed by citizens. A civic republican wing combines the right to an asset with a duty of a citizen to behave in a particular way. Perhaps the main difference that arises between these liberal and civic republican conceptions concerns whether or not restrictions are imposed on how assets are used. Liberal accounts do not specify that assets should be used in a particular way. This allows the possibility of 'stakeblowing', that is people blowing any assets they hold on 'inappropriate' things such as getting drunk. In contrast, civic republicans insist that assets should only be used for certain valuable purposes.

This chapter is organised as follows. First, I set out the assumptions underpinning the most developed models within the liberal and civic republican traditions. I concentrate on Bruce Ackerman and Anne Alstott's model of stakeholding within the liberal tradition and Stuart White's account of democratic mutual regard within the civic republican tradition. Second, I highlight the key difference that emerges between different versions of citizenship, namely whether citizens are free to use their assets however they please or whether they can only use their assets in specified ways. Third, I look at different wealth taxes as a way of funding assets. A common emphasis across both liberal and civic republican versions of the assets agenda is using a wealth tax to pay for assets. Fourth, I examine criticisms as well as an alternative to an assets approach.

Equality and liberty

A common starting point across different models of citizenship is an emphasis on equality as a foundation for freedom. Whatever their other differences, liberal and civic republican models believe in the importance of equality as an underpinning for freedom. Models of assets are usually concerned with individual freedom, allowing people to select and pursue their own life-plans and goals. However, advocates of stakes insist that it is not possible to pursue such goals without access to material resources. The uneven distribution of wealth is thought to deny people of the resources they need to pursue their goals. Those without adequate resources have to depend on others, and this condition undermines the capacity to follow their own plans and goals. Equality is seen as important for securing the conditions under which individual freedom can flourish. Stuart White comments that, 'Egalitarian politics seeks to eliminate the conditions of dependency, the conditions of living at the mercy of others, and is therefore centrally concerned with making lives freer' (White 2002, 36).

Equality and liberty are seen as complementary values. This runs counter to an important strand within recent political theory that suggests that values such as equality and liberty are often in conflict. For example, individuals such as Isaiah Berlin (1958) and John Gray (2000) argue that social and political life is characterised by 'value pluralism' – the existence of a plurality of values such as equality, liberty, community and responsibility. These commentators continue that many of these values clash, and there is no rational way of deciding how these conflicts should be resolved. A tragedy of life is that we are forced to make choices about what values to adopt although we lack an adequate basis to do this. Although advocates of stakeholding are alert to the tensions that exist between liberty and equality, they insist that these values are fundamentally compatible. For example, Stuart White (2002) argues that caution has to be taken over the claims of value pluralism. He says that an apparent conflict of values might disappear upon closer inspection, or that where a conflict does exist there might be reasons for preferring one value rather than the other. White continues that equality and liberty provides an example where values are complementary. Bruce Ackerman and Anne Alstott (1999) argue that, 'We reject the idea that there is an inexorable tradeoff between liberty and equality. The stakeholder society promises more of both' (Ackerman and Alstott 1999, 4).

Liberal citizenship

Although there is agreement that equality is important for freedom, different models exist within the realm of citizenship. Bruce

Ackerman and Anne Alstott (1999) set out the most cogent liberal model of asset-ownership.[1] Bruce Ackerman (2003) argues that the themes set out in his book *Social Justice in the Liberal State* provides the intellectual background for the $80,000 grant. In *Social Justice in the Liberal State*, Ackerman aims to set out the conditions associated with the legitimate exercise of power. He argues that power is an inescapable and pervasive feature of human life, and this gives rise to the question of how such power can be justified. Ackerman says that 'conversational liberalism' is the best way of conferring legitimacy on to power. The idea is that the exercise of power is legitimate if the wielder can justify this to other people in a conversation constrained by three principles. First, the discussion must be rational in the sense that a person must provide a reason for the exercise of power rather than merely trying to suppress or stunt debate. Second, conversation should be consistent, which means that the reasons put forward to justify power should not be inconsistent with reasons used to justify other exercises of power. Third, conversation should be neutral which implies that no reason is a good reason if it involves a person asserting that their conception of the good is better than that advanced by anyone else, or that he or she is inherently superior to other citizens. Ackerman says that these principles combine to form a model of constrained conversation or neutral discussion.

Ackerman argues that the emphasis on constrained conversation creates a bias towards equality in the initial material endowments possessed by individuals. He writes that, 'Since I'm at least as good as you are, I should get at least as much of the stuff we both desire – at least until you give me some neutral reason for getting more' (Ackerman 1980, 58). Ackerman says that the neutrality principle which implies that no person or conception of the good is intrinsically superior to anyone or anything else means that each person is at least as good as other people. This places the burden of proof upon those who wish to have a greater share of initial material resources than their peers. Ackerman says that conversational liberalism permits the pursuit of different lifestyles. He continues that while his account of liberalism acknowledges the importance of diversity, there is a presumption that people should have an equal start in life.

As part of this discussion, Ackerman considers differences in the genetic endowments possessed by different people. He considers a situation in which natural talents are distributed differently among a population. For example, he says that one person may have a genetic disposition to be good at mathematics and that a different person may have a natural talent for empathy. Ackerman continues that the talent for mathematics might command greater reward in the marketplace than empathy. Given this, he asks whether the person who lacks a talent for mathematics is justified in asking for compensation from the state, in terms perhaps of a greater share of initial resources. Ackerman rejects calls for compensation, arguing that it violates the neutrality principle by suggesting that certain ways of living are intrinsically superior to another. He says that as long as people have some advantage in the talents that they possess, conversational liberalism endorses the development of a range of talents. In a recent statement of this position, he writes that, 'Bound by the principle of Neutrality, no government official can ever award B compensation on the grounds that his maths-poor/empathy-rich genes make him worse off than A; and vice versa. In the eyes of the liberal state, the genetic equipment provided to A is no worse off than that provided to B, and neither has a legitimate complaint of injustice' (Ackerman 2003, 176). Ackerman makes a limited exception to this in those cases where people lack any comparative advantage in the distribution of talents. He says that certain categories of the disabled may qualify under this heading, and as a result could call for special compensation. His main thrust, however, is against such interventions.

Stakeholder grant

The payment of the grant to 21 year olds as a right of citizenship chimes with the emphasis on equality of initial material resources. Ackerman and Alstott say that although their ultimate aim is to provide the grant to all US citizens when they turn 21, in the initial stages the stake should only be provided to those citizens who have lived at least 11 years in the United States. They say that paying the stake to all US citizens free of this additional residency requirement would mean that the grant would be made available to two categories of people that are likely to provoke public disquiet. On the one hand, 'birthright citizens' who have been born in the United States – and thus would qualify for US citizenship – but have never lived or intend to live in the United States. They suggest that public support for the scheme is likely to dissipate with well publicised cases of those people who were born in the United States but lived all their life abroad turning up in the United States just before their 21ˢᵗ birthday in order to collect their $80,000 grant before returning home. On the other hand, they say that the public is unlikely to countenance providing newly arrived immigrants who become citizens with an $80,000 stake when they turn 21. Ackerman and Alstott continue that even if the public would allow such payments, this might lead to pressures to rein in immigration. Ackerman and Alstott say that they would rather constrain eligibility for grant payments in the short and medium run than risk the chance that the shutters would start coming down on immigration. Ackerman and Alstott say that their main aim is to get the grant established, and once the scheme is up and running there may be potential for relaxing this residency requirement.[2]

Third way

Ackerman and Alstott say that while the stakeholder grant can be treated in isolation from other measures, they hope it would be the first in a series of other policies designed to promote free and equal citizenship. For example, they support paying individuals a citizens' pension that will not be related to previous employment history. By ensuring that people do not receive a higher pension simply because they have been more active in the workplace than those individuals who have been less active, the citizens' pension will help guarantee that the state is neutral between those people who chose to work in paid employment and those people who did otherwise. Ackerman and Alstott note that such a policy would benefit those women who had to shoulder the bulk of unpaid domestic labour within the household.

Bruce Ackerman and Anne Alstott say that the stakeholder grant represents a step towards their broader ambition of implementing a 'third way' in public policy. Ackerman and Alstott argue that two different visions have dominated how American government is seen in recent times. First, a 'welfarist' mindset which sees that the job of government is to take care and maximise the welfare of its citizens. This usually involves the state making decisions on behalf of citizens. They say that this implies the state engages in paternalistic social engineering. Second, a 'libertarian' model of society that attempts to roll back the frontiers of the state as far as possible. This standpoint rejects the idea that government has a right to tax and redistribute resources. Ackerman and Alstott criticise welfarism because it does not allow citizens sufficient space to make decisions. They write that the, 'point of stakeholding is to liberate each citizen from government, not to create an excuse for a vast new bureaucracy intervening in our lives' (Ackerman and Alstott 1999, 9). They argue that the libertarian view is flawed because it fails to recognise that equality is needed if freedom is to flourish. Thus, while Ackerman and Alstott do not reject the idea of significant public intervention, they believe it should not be through centralised or statist institutions. This points to a decentralised political system. The attempt to find an alternative to centralisation helps explain the size of their grant proposal. In particular, if a grant is to help create an alternative to a paternalistic state, empowering people to make the decisions that bear directly on their own lives, then the size of any endowment should be substantial. They suggest that $80,000 would enable a person to have significant control over their own life.

Civic republican citizenship

Civic republican models see asset-ownership as important for life within the republic. Stuart White (2003; 2006a) is a recent advocate of this strand of thinking. He views asset-ownership as, 'part of a much larger package of reforms aimed at establishing a progressive, "neo-republican" form of political economy' (White 2006a, 1). His case for assets springs from a commitment to democratic mutual regard. This means that, when citizens come together to decide the institutions and laws that govern their lives they view, 'one another as equals, and possessing certain basic interests that these institutions must respect and protect' (White 2003, 27). Citizens thus show each other a measure of respect. Mutual regard in itself need not be conducted on an egalitarian basis. White notes that it is possible that a master and slave show each other respect. This is a hierarchical conception of mutual regard, and so to underline that individuals should enjoy an equality of status in their dealings with each other, he proposes a model of *democratic* mutual regard. White uses this formulation to derive a set of principles that ought to govern a just society. He says that recognising that people have basic interests in common raises the issue of the content of these interests. In terms of interests he distinguishes between integrity and opportunity interests. Integrity broadly supports allowing people to live a life in accordance with the way they think that life ought to be best lived. This permits people to enjoy physical integrity (not being subject to unwarranted physical intrusion by others). White also says integrity allows people to express opinions about the way that they think their own life is best lived, as well as being able to reflect and alter these opinions over time. In relation to opportunity, White says that people should have access to goods that impinge on their well being (such as health) as well as those goods that enable them to achieve their own goals and commitments. White says that 'brute luck' circumstances constitute an important barrier to guaranteeing well-being and agency. He notes that brute luck refers to sources of disadvantage over which an individual cannot exert control. He draws attention to three important types of brute luck disadvantage. First, those inequalities in initial endowments or wealth-holdings as a result of being born into a rich family. Second, a genetic lottery that distributes marketable talents throughout society. People have different marketable talents, and these different talents are allocated randomly by nature. People who possess talents that have low market value are subject to bad brute luck in the marketplace. A third source of brute luck disadvantage consists of being born with substantial physical or mental handicaps, again as a result of a genetic lottery. White argues that justice demands that public policy should attempt to correct these brute luck disadvantages. White also endorses efforts to stem vulnerability. This aims to address the exploitation that potentially occurs when one person is dependent on another. The independent person may use their power over another individual as an opportunity to extract some advantage.

Alongside integrity, opportunity and non-vulnerability, White advocates a reciprocity principle which states roughly and broadly that, 'people who are willing to share in the social product (the flow of goods and services intentionally generated by the combined industry of the members of a society) ought to make a return for this in the form of a relevantly proportional productive contribution of their own (White 2003, 50). White argues that if people are willing to enjoy the benefits of social co-operation but are unprepared to help generate this social product, then these individuals are guilty of exploiting those who do make such a contribution. This occurs because non-contributors free-ride on the contributions made by others. White argues that this exploitation is a source of injustice, and rectifying this requires individuals to make a contribution of their own. He continues that this reciprocity principle can take two main forms. A 'strictly proportionate' version requires that the individual make a contribution that is strictly proportional to the value of the social product that they extract for themselves. White argues that an important problem with this conception of reciprocity is that this version has an inegalitarian bias. In particular, people do not have the same capacity or ability to make a productive contribution. If one links benefits strictly to contributions, then this means that those people who have a greater capacity to make a productive contribution will be able to claim a greater share of the social product. As greater capacity is a type of brute luck, this means that a strictly proportionate type of reciprocity will allow brute luck inequalities to emerge. In contrast with this, White favours a 'fair dues' model of reciprocity. This conception says that within the context of arrangements that meet the other demands of justice to an appropriate extent, and as a result of this would provide individuals with good opportunities for productive contributions, people who claim a share of the benefits of social co-operation in these circumstances should be required to make a contribution in return.

White outlines a series of policies designed to promote his notion of democratic mutual regard. One of the most prominent of these policies involves the payment of a 'basic capital' grant. We have seen that White's concept of fair reciprocity involves steps being taken to eradicate the adverse consequences of brute luck. One aspect of this relates to the unequal distribution of wealth due to inheritance. The provision of capital grants is aimed at introducing greater equality in this pattern of wealth-holding and providing a correction against the bad luck of being born into poor circumstances. Drawing on Alexis De Tocqueville, White (2006b) says that one of the dangers of a property-owning democracy is that it could foster individualism within society. Property-ownership might encourage citizens to see themselves apart from others rather than recognising their ties with others. White says that this creates a potential problem for reciprocity because this is based on acknowledging the links that people have with each other, while individualism tends to erode these ties. He says that this problem could be compounded as individual ownership might also support a materialistic outlook as people seek to concentrate only on their material interests. White argues that a society based simply on property-ownership might not be stable as it would be torn by individualism and materialism. He argues that Tocqueville's analysis of civil society, however, suggests a possible way that these ills might be combated. In particular, participation within self-governing associations could temper individualism by making people aware of their connections with others. Furthermore, participation in public forums could impel people to justify their claims on resources, which might clip their materialist instincts.

Restrictions

Both the liberal and civic republican models, discussed above, propose providing a capital grant to individuals as an element of citizenship. Capital grants are the main type of asset proposed within the field of citizenship. The arguments used to justify asset-ownership within citizenship create a tendency to focus on capital grants rather than other types of assets. In particular, models of citizenship emphasise the importance of material resources for citizenship. As material resources are centrally about money, both liberal and civic republican models emphasise the significance of stocks of money or capital grants. Perhaps the main difference that exists between the liberal and civic republican strands concerns whether or not restrictions are imposed on how assets are used. The different stances towards restrictions reflect different attitudes towards 'stakeblowing'. People could use their capital grant in a variety of ways. One possibility is that people might simply 'blow' their grant on frivolous or seemingly wasteful activities. For example, a 21 year old coming into $80,000 might decide to spend all this money on a big party for his or her friends. This is not to say everyone will behave in this fashion. A majority of individuals might in fact use their stake 'wisely', for example by paying for education. However, the possibility remains that some people will fritter away their stakes. One obvious way of trying to prevent stake-blowing is to impose restrictions on how assets are used. Thus, people might only be allowed to use a capital grant for paying for education or starting a business and not for things such as having a big party. Broadly speaking, liberal citizenship emphasises the importance of rights to basic capital and does not impose restrictions on how the grant is spent. Civic republicans ally the provision of a grant to a duty to use it wisely. This lends weight to placing restrictions on how the grant is used.

Bruce Ackerman and Anne Alstott are opposed to imposing any sort of restrictions on how the $80,000 stake can be used. They write that, 'Stakeholders are free. They may use their money for any purpose they choose: to start a business or pay for more education, to buy a house or raise a family or save for the future. But they must take responsibility for their choices. Their triumphs and blunders are their own' (Ackerman and Alstott 1999, 5). This opposition to restrictions on use flows directly from the notion of a conversational liberalism. The attempt by the state to restrict the options pursued by people violates the neutrality principle because it suggests that a particular conception of the good is inherently superior to other notions. The commitment that conversational liberalism exhibits towards diversity is in harmony with a stance that does not place restrictions on how the grant is spent.

Although Ackerman and Alstott insist that people should ultimately be allowed to use their stakes as they wish, they recognise that individuals would benefit more if their assets are used wisely rather than unwisely. Rather than placing conditions on how their grant is used, they suggest that their grant should only be made available to those who have graduated with a high school diploma. Graduation from high school implies a certain level of education, and it is hoped that this education will dispose people to use their $80,000 stake wisely. Ackerman and Alstott also say that the $80,000 stake could be paid in tranches of $20,000 until a person's early twenties. They believe that staggering the grant reduces the possibility that a person will blow all their stake in one go by creating time for them to reflect on their spending decisions.

In contrast to Ackerman and Alstott, Stuart White favours placing restrictions on how assets are used as a way of averting stake-blowing. White argues that while people should be provided with the material endowments they need to lead an autonomous life, the collective provision of these assets imposes a reciprocal obligation to use these assets wisely. The principle of reciprocity is manifested through the asset being used on valuable purposes. He comments that, 'On maturity each citizen will be eligible for a sizeable capital grant. The individual will be free to use this endowment to finance a range of activities broadly related to productive participation in the community, for example, to finance courses of higher education or vocational training, to establish a new business, to finance the costs of moving to a new area in search of employment, or perhaps to subsidize time off from employment to care for dependants' (White 2003, 186). The view that assets should ideally only be used for particular purposes is part of a broader civic republican injunction that individuals have a duty or obligation to behave in particular ways.

Stuart White rejects the idea that restrictions on eligibility provide a desirable alternative to restrictions on use. Will Paxton and Stuart White (2006) argue that restricting grants to those who have graduated with a high school diploma threatens the universal nature of capital grants in alarming ways. They contend that many of those who are likely to be excluded are precisely those individuals that this grant is intended to help, namely those individuals from poorer backgrounds. Will Paxton and Stuart White argue that while restrictions on use can be justified as a matter of principle, there may be important obstacles to putting this into practice. They say that it may be difficult for government to implement a set of regulations in the system of provision. For example, restrictions that involve training might be linked with fraud as students sign up and pay for courses that turn out to be bogus or sub-standard. Paxton and White say that determined individuals could also probably get around restrictions. For example, a stakeholder might purchase tools as part of a business plan and the sell the tools immediately afterwards for cash. Paxton and White conclude that such practical difficulties mean that full-blown restrictions are probably not viable.

Will Paxton and Stuart White suggest that education and advice could be used as an alternative to formal restrictions on use. The hope here is that education would teach people how to use their assets wisely and responsibly. Paxton and White say that a programme of education could combine three elements. First, general education in schools. Young people could be taught the basics of financial education. Regular financial statements could be provided to keep young people alert of their accounts. Second, supportive advice just before the asset matures. They say that young people could be provided with advice in a one-to-one session as they enter their late teens. Paxton and White suggest this advice could be supplied by a teacher or an advisor who works within the local council's youth service. They say that they back an approach that either makes this advice session voluntary, or, more stringently, insists that access to the asset is dependent upon having attended an advice session. These authors write that general education and supportive advice would be made available to all. Paxton and White continue that a third component could involve targeted mentoring for people who require special assistance. Mentorship would be provided to those with special needs, for example young people in local authority care homes. Mentors could be provided by those professionals already in contact with these young people, for example social workers for those in care.

The emphasis that Stuart White, Bruce Ackerman and Anne Alstott all place on education as a way of avoiding stakeblowing indicates that although important differences exist between the different models at a philosophical level, these differences lessen at a practical level. Thus, although Stuart White believes that there is a case for restrictions on use, he concedes that full-blown restrictions are unlikely to be a feasible policy option. Similarly, although Ackerman and Alstott are against placing restrictions on use, they nevertheless endorse steps to reduce the possibility of stakeblowing. This is not to say that all differences disappear at a practical level. Ackerman, Alstott and White use education as a means of tackling stakeblowing but differ over the role played by education. Ackerman and Alstott use education as a filter to decide whether or not a person should get access to a $80,000 grant, and so education is important before they receive a stake. Paxton and White spotlight the role of education once a person has already received a stake and is about to make decisions about how to use it.

Wealth taxes

As with social policy, providing material stakes for citizens incurs significant costs. For example, Bruce Ackerman and Anne Alstott argue that introducing their $80,000 stakeholder grant would cost a substantial amount of money. Using data for 1997, they say that around 3.1 million US citizens would be eligible for the $80,000 grant at 21 years of age. They say that providing grants to all these people would cost roughly $255 billion. Ackerman and Alstott note that in 1998, total expenditure by the United States federal government was approximately $1.7 trillion. This means that providing a system of stakeholder grants would increase federal spending to $2 trillion, which amounts roughly to a 15 per cent increase in federal spending. Ackerman and Alstott continue that by 2011, stakeholder grants could be made available to around 4 million young people. This would raise the cost of their stakeholder proposal in 2011 to $320 billion.

Both the liberal and civic republican models discussed above advocate using a wealth tax to pay for capital grants. This commitment to wealth taxes usually flows from the arguments used to justify a policy of providing stakes to individuals. For example, Bruce Ackerman and Anne Alstott (1999) say that they are happy for grants to be paid for through income tax or cuts in public spending elsewhere, they favour using wealth taxes to pay for stakes. They say that the principal source of funds for their $80,000 stake is a 'trusteeship tax' that is imposed on the estates of stakeholders. Ackerman and Alstott argue that justice demands that resources that people claim in order to give them an equal start in life imposes an obligation on them to ensure the same assistance is provided to future generations. These authors say that when stakeholders pass away, they will face an obligation to put money into a national fund which will be used to pay for the next generation of stakeholders. They say that the aim of the scheme should be self-financing, with the payback obligations either covering the total costs of providing grants to the next generation of stakeholders or allowing a modest surplus to be made which can be used to increase the value of the grants. Although Ackerman and Alstott hopes that their scheme should be self-financing, they state that grants might have to draw on additional sources of funding, particularly during the early stages of the policy. They advocate a 2 per cent tax on all wealth to help pay for the stakes, writing that the, 'tie between wealthholding and stakeholding expresses a fundamental social responsibility. Every American has an obligation to contribute to a fair starting point for all' (Ackerman and Alstott 1999, 4–5). Stuart White (2003) endorses taxes on the transfer of wealth as a product of the principles of equality, reciprocity and democratic mutual regard. He believes that inheritances can be a source of brute luck inequality and as such should be subject to correction. He adds that large inheritances means that a person may be in a position where they can enjoy the product of social co-operation without making a relevant contribution to this product. This violates the principle of reciprocity. Finally, unequal inheritances can contribute to class inequality which undermines the achievement of a society based on democratic mutual regard. Stuart White argues that tackling these issues means that a comprehensive tax should be placed on the gifts or bequests that a person receives.

The link between wealth taxes and assets is in fact a recurrent theme in the literature on assets within the field of citizenship. Of course, support for a wealth tax extends beyond those interested in asset ownership. It is possible to advocate taxing wealth without also supporting an assets agenda. While wealth taxes and assets can be separated, stress is nevertheless placed on wealth taxes in the citizenship wing of the assets agenda.

While there is a common emphasis on wealth taxes, these taxes can be designed in a range of ways (Atkinson 1972; Commission on Taxation and Citizenship 2000). One option is to tax the income accruing from wealth. Stocks of wealth can create returns. For example, property let out to tenants yields rental income, and shares usually generate dividend payments. Taxes would then be placed on rents or dividend payments. The main disadvantage of this type of tax is that it leaves the underlying distribution of wealth untouched, and so can only play a limited role in tackling wealth inequality. Consequently, most models of assets prefer the other main types of wealth tax, namely placing a tax on transfers of wealth or taxes on the underlying stock of wealth.

Taxing transfers of wealth

Perhaps the most popular type of wealth tax within the assets agenda is a tax on transfers of wealth. Stuart White argues above that transfers of wealth constitute a source of brute luck inequality, and so should be taxed. Transfers of wealth are an important way that advantage is passed from one generation to the next (Bowles, Gintis and Osborne Groves 2005). Liberals are drawn to taxing these transfers as a way of pursuing their aim of securing free and equal citizenship for all.

Taxes on transfers can be shaped in different ways. One type of wealth transfer occurs when someone dies. A person's estate is then transferred to others, as when a parent bequeaths an estate for their children. Transfers of wealth can also occur when an individual provides a gift to another person when they are both living. Different taxes can be fashioned depending whether they concentrate on either bequests or gifts, or focus on both bequests and gifts. Also important is whether a tax is placed on a donor or recipient of a wealth transfer. If a tax is imposed on the donor, then the tax will apply to the total amount transferred by the person. If the tax is targeted at the recipient, then only that part of wealth that they receive is liable to tax. For transfers of wealth at death, if a tax is imposed on a donor (an estates tax), then the whole of a person's estate is liable for tax. If a tax is placed on a recipient (an inheritance tax), then only that part of wealth that they inherit (say a tenth of the whole estate) is susceptible to tax.

A number of commentators favour placing a tax on the recipient rather than the donor of a wealth transfer (Atkinson 1972; Commission on Taxation and Citizenship 2000; Maxwell 2004). This allows the tax gathering authorities to take into account the financial circumstances of the recipient when setting the tax. One prominent proposal is to have some form of capital receipts tax that covers both inheritances and gifts. For example, Anthony Atkinson and Commission on Taxation and Citizenship advocate a lifetime capital receipts tax that places a tax on the total value of gifts and inheritances that a person receives over their lifetime. They say this lifetime tax is easier to administer than a version that collects a capital receipts tax annually.

Taxing stocks of wealth: land value taxation

Apart from taxing wealth, the most common type of wealth tax used in the assets agenda is to tax the stock of wealth. One example of this that has attracted contemporary interest is a tax placed on the value of land (Maxwell and Vigor 2005; Wilcox 2005; McLean 2006a; 2006b). Land value taxation has been the subject of long-standing concern. Henry George (1932) suggests that land is the most important factor of production, overshadowing both labour and capital. He suggests that it is the foundation upon which labour and capital operate, and is central for production. He continues that the bulk of material progress is captured by rents for land rather than the returns to labour or capital (that is wages or interest). George contends that tackling the unequal distribution of wealth requires some form of common property. He says that it is unnecessary to abolish private property to tackle inequality due to unequal ownership of land. He says that this can be achieved by placing a tax on the value of land and rents associated with land. He recommends this policy because he states that this builds on existing institutions rather than requiring a whole new machinery of government. More recently Iain McLean (2006b) argues that land value taxation is a just and efficient way of raising public money. He says that the value of land derives from three main sources, namely its scarcity, the value added by the land-owner and the activities of public authorities. McLean argues that most of the value of land today comes from the first and third of these sources. For example, the money that central and local government invest in the transport infrastructure in a particular area adds a premium on land. Thus land values rise when an underground tube link is built in the area. McLean argues that the fact that the value added to land comes from sources other than the activities of the landowner provides a rationale for taxing the value of land. Moreover, a tax on land values will tend to have a less distortionary impact on economic activity than the imposition of other taxes.

Although land tax has provoked interest, there is resistance to using taxes on the stock of wealth as the main basis for funding assets. One criticism is that such taxes is likely to be costly to administer. This will require public authorities to make a regular assessment of all wealth, financial and non-financial, that a person owns, and the costs of gathering this information is probably sizeable. The costs will tend to increase the smaller the interval between the assessments of wealth. Furthermore, some say that such a tax will probably be subject to avoidance as people will seek to shift their wealth into forms that may avoid taxation. The Commission on Taxation and Citizenship (2000) notes that rich people may be tempted to move financial wealth into off-shore accounts in order to avoid taxation. Ethical concerns are also raised alongside these efficiency considerations. Anthony Atkinson (1972) says that such a tax does not distinguish between accumulated and inherited wealth. Accumulated wealth refers to wealth that a person has acquired by his or her own efforts. Inherited wealth is wealth that has been transferred to an individual, either in the shape of a gift or through an inheritance. Atkinson says that while fairness dictates that there is a case for allowing accumulated wealth, there is little to be said for inherited wealth. The failure of a tax on the stocks of wealth to separate out the accumulated and inherited components means that it can be questioned on grounds of justice.

Alternative to wealth taxes: the community fund

Models of citizenship do not rely exclusively on wealth taxes to pay for assets. Stuart White (2003) notes that a community fund idea can be found in the writings of commentators such as James Meade and Gerald Holtham. The basic idea is that government would create a pot of money on behalf of the community. The government would then employ an independent set of financial advisors to invest this pot of money for the nation. The returns to these investments would be used to replenish the fund in future years as well as pay for various good causes. James Meade (1989) argues that a just society involves paying everyone an annual income payment or social dividend from government. He suggests that part of this might be funded by government taking ownership of half the wealth of the community and investing this on the stock exchange. The returns to this investment would help pay for this dividend. Gerald Holtham (1999) argues that a national patrimony could be created that would help fund spending in health and education. Holtham argues that to protect the community fund being manipulated by politicians, government should set up a board of trustees from outside the political arena who would then delegate the running of the fund to private equity managers. Holtham notes that since the 1950s the real rate of return of shares in Britain has averaged about 6 per cent a year, and so the community fund should generate a substantial sum to spend on health and education. Stuart White (2003; 2006) argues that a community fund could be used to pay for a citizen's stake. He says that such a scheme would mean that collective ownership would be used in service of individual ownership.

Such a pot of money would require initial start-up funds to get it up and running. Once the initial funds were invested, the pot should be self-financing. There are a variety of ways of raising the start-up funds. Gerald Holtham (1999) says that in Britain £50 billion could be raised by taxes on capital, for example by closing loopholes in the system of inheritance tax and diverting this money for the collective fund. Stuart White (2006) suggests that start-up money could be gained through an auction of rights to use spectrum space for telecommunications firms. He states that in 2000 the British government raised £35 billion through such an auction.

Earmarking

One suggestion made within the literature on assets is to use 'earmarking' to increase support for paying for assets. Earmarking explicitly links a source of revenue with a particular spending programme. The Commission on Taxation and Citizenship (2000) proposes that the revenue raised from a capital receipts tax should be earmarked for universal capital grants for young people. Earmarking is suggested as a way of increasing public support for the taxes they pay. The Commission on Taxation and Citizenship notes that its investigation of public attitudes towards taxation reveals that members of the public feel a sense of disconnection with the taxes they pay, being unclear about what their taxes are spent on. The Commission says that earmarking could be used to link taxes to expenditure. The Commission notes that there are a variety of ways that earmarking may be shaped. In a strictly hypothecated version, all the money for a particular spending programme comes from a specially designated tax. A less stringent version of earmarking does not insist that the proceeds from a particular tax should pay for the whole of a particular spending programme. Instead, earmarking could yield funds that contribute part of the payment for a particular spending programme. The remainder of the funds would come from elsewhere. The Commission proposes that money from a capital receipts tax could be earmarked for capital grants for young people.

Although earmarking potentially helps reduce public resistance to paying taxes in general, and quell opposition to inheritance taxes in particular, earmarking does not guarantee that citizens will feel connected to the taxes they pay. If there is widespread distrust of politicians among the general population, then large swathes of the public may not believe that the government will spend taxes on their stated purposes. Added to this is the main disadvantage of earmarking, namely a loss of flexibility over government revenues. Government has less flexibility in allocating resources when taxes are earmarked than when all taxes are placed into a general pot that pays for all government spending. The financial requirements of any government programme are likely to change according to circumstances. It is difficult for earmarking to track all these shifts, which means that earmarking might provide too little or too much. While the problem is greatest for models that stress strict hypothecation, this problem affects all models of earmarking. In situations where spending plans have to alter significantly, government might find that earmarking compounds the disconnection that people feel over how their taxes are spent.

Earmarking is thus subject to conflicting arguments. Miranda Lewis and Stuart White (2006) explore the Commission on Taxation and Citizenship's ear-marking proposal in their examination of public attitudes towards inheritance tax. As part of their study, these researchers asked their respondents on their view about using an earmarked wealth tax to pay for one of the three spending programmes, namely a more generous Child Trust Fund; general support programmes for young children (such as Sure Start – that is centres based on communities that provide facilities such as crèches and classes for parents with young children); or policies aimed at improving long-term care for the elderly (such as nursing homes). Lewis and White found that while their participants responded positively to the general idea of earmarking, there were differing views about what any earmarked wealth tax should be spent on. In particular, they say that linking spending to the long-term care of the elderly elicited the greatest support and the Child Trust Fund the least support. They continue that while people found it difficult to make an intuitive link between an inheritance tax and the provision of a child's inheritance, one such link did exist between inheritance tax and the elderly. In particular, as the elderly were targeted by an inheritance tax, they should benefit in some way from the earmarked tax. Thus, while earmarking might generate support as a way of paying for asset policies, this should be set against the possible desire that any earmarked money should be spent elsewhere.

Criticisms of capital grants

The capital grant proposals discussed above provoke criticism and debate within the academic community. Cécile Fabre (2003) argues that policies such as capital grants raise issues of serious concern for those interested in equality. She raises several complaints. First, capital grants do not take adequate account of those born with expensive tastes or preferences. She argues that advocates of stakeholding believe that by introducing greater equality on the endowments possessed by individuals, there is greater likelihood that any inequalities that arise between people are the result of choice not luck. Fabre contends, however, that the choices that people express may be the result of preferences over which they have little or no control. Some people may be unlucky to be born with expensive tastes, preferring an expensive hobby of photography say to a cheap pastime of fishing. Those with expensive tastes will need a greater share of resources to reach a similar level of welfare and well-being than those with inexpensive preferences. Fabre says that the luck based inequalities that result here are not fair. Second, capital grants do not take into account the need of redistribution over a person's lifetime. She states that paying a capital grant at one point in a person's life does not address the point that people need additional resources at special events during their life. For example, extra resources are needed if one is getting married or to help cope with the birth of a child. The failure of grants to present such resources means that this policy is inadequate from a lifecycle perspective. Fabre argues that Individual Development Accounts perform better than capital grants in this regard. For example, by allowing for redistribution over a lifecycle, IDAs permit people to have access to the extra resources they need at important events over their lifetime (though as we shall see in the next chapter, Fabre has other egalitarian criticisms of IDAs). Third, Fabre says that capital grants do not take into account the different natural talents possessed by individuals. This means that those who lack such talents will be able to use the grant as a source of brute luck material advantage over those who lack such talents.

Part of Fabre's critique represents a difference of philosophical principle between herself and the assets agenda. Her emphasis on fashioning policy to take account of expensive tastes is philosophically opposed to Bruce Ackerman's insistence that neutrality demands that government must not take into account expensive preferences. He says that a person who prefers photography rather than fishing, 'can't expect the liberal state to increase his citizen-stake on the ground that photography is especially worthy of state support – such a rationale is a plain offence to the Neutrality principle' (Ackerman 2003, 183). There is little prospect for bridging the gap between these principles and ultimately one is forced to choose one or the other of these principles.

This philosophical difference does not exist for the civic republican version of the assets agenda discussed above. Stuart White marks the commitment to tackle brute luck inequality a feature of his account of democratic mutual regard. Thus, White shares Fabre's emphasis on tackling brute luck. Although White does not make expensive tastes an explicit part of his account of capital grants, his model is capable in theory of being extended to allow special compensation to be paid with those with expensive tastes. Of course, in practice it may not be easy to identify and implement a system that is fully sensitive to individual preferences, and administering such a system will be more expensive than implementing a uniform system.

Fabre's point about lifecycle redistribution is more open to challenge than her argument about expensive tastes. Chapter 1 noted that in Sweden one key argument for assets is that this will improve the welfare system by constituting a more efficient way of redistributing income over the lifecycle rather than relying on government tax revenues. Within asset-based welfare at least there is direct concern with the importance of lifecycle redistribution. Within citizenship, the size of the capital grant typically endorsed allows for significant redistribution over the lifecycle. For example, although Ackerman and Alstott do not make lifecycle payments a feature of their scheme as doing so would fall foul of their neutrality principle, the size of the $80,000 stake is substantial enough to accommodate significant lifecycle payments should a person wish to spend it in this fashion. A person is not committed to have to spend the whole stake at once. A stakeholder might spend $40,000 immediately, but keep the remainder for later dates. A civic republican version of capital grants could be fashioned which integrates some lifecycle characteristics, for example, by stipulating that one of the purposes of a capital grant is to help save for one's retirement.

Basic income versus basic capital

Criticisms of capital grants are sometimes combined with the discussion of an alternative policy for securing individual freedom. This focuses on how a different policy might be better placed to achieve the aims of basic capital. These debates are usually about a 'basic income' versus 'basic capital'. Basic income means citizens are entitled to receive an income payment at regular intervals, typically annually. As with asset policies, basic income can be developed in liberal and civic republican directions. Liberal citizenship tends to endorse an unconditional basic income which means that no conditions are imposed on how they spend their income. In addition, the receipt of basic income is unrelated to any other conditions besides being a citizen, such as one's record of current or previous employment (Fitzpatrick 1999). Republican citizenship imposes conditions on basic income payments. For example, a participatory income might be instituted which ties income payments to an obligation to find work or conduct service in the community.

Basic income and basic capital are related proposals. Bruce Ackerman and Anne Alstott say that their $80,000 stake and basic income belong to the same family of policies (Ackerman and Alstott 1999). It is possible to save all the regular income payments one receives into the equivalent of a capital grant. Alternatively, one can convert a large stock of money into a flow of smaller regular income payments. One option when considering basic capital alongside basic income is to combine them in a policy programme. Thomas Paine supported both policies when he proposed that 21 year olds should receive a capital grant and those aged 50 or over should receive an annual income. More recently Bruce Ackerman and Anne Alstott advocate a stakeholder grant and a citizen's pension.

Although one might combine both basic income and basic capital, a significant portion of academic debates nonetheless consists of comparing basic income with basic capital. The purpose of this comparison is to explore which type of policy is best placed to meet various objectives. Two main arguments are advanced for a basic income over basic capital. First, basic income provides better protection against stakeblowing than a basic capital (Fitzpatrick 1999). According to this view, providing people with a one-off grant means that if a person blows the whole of their grant in one go, then there is little they can do to reverse the consequences of this decision. A person may decide to blow their stake, but then come to regret this later. However, nothing can be changed once this grant is spent. In contrast, basic income allows people to change their mind. If a person blows some of their basic income payments and comes to regret this, then there is always an opportunity to make different decisions with their later payments.

Second, some commentators suggest that a basic income is better placed than capital grants in underpinning democracy. Carol Pateman (2003; 2004) contrasts 'political freedom' which concerns self-government or autonomy with 'economic freedom' which concentrates on individual opportunity. She argues that a healthy democracy requires political rather than economic freedom. Pateman says that basic income is superior to capital grants in promoting political freedom, and hence democracy, because it breaks a link between citizenship and employment. She states that a, 'crucial difference between basic income and stakeholding, is that a basic income would give citizens the freedom not to be employed' (Pateman 2004, 96). She says that such a policy will particularly benefit women, as many women have not enjoyed the full fruits of citizenship because females typically perform the bulk of unpaid domestic labour in households (child-rearing, cooking, cleaning and so on).

Supporters of assets can respond to the stakeblowing objection in two main ways. The first response directly confronts the stakeblowing point. This involves highlighting the measures taken within basic capital models to address stakeblowing. Civic republicans deploy restrictions on use to prevent people from wasting their stakes. The liberal model discussed above emphasises restrictions on eligibility as well as staggering the $80,000 grant into four $20,000 payments. Thus the issue is not that basic income addresses stakeblowing while basic capital ignores this phenomenon but rather whether basic income or basic capital is more effective at overcoming stakeblowing. It is an empirical question as to whether basic income is better placed than the different versions of the assets agenda in combating stakeblowing.

A second response is to say that the emphasis on stakeblowing should be offset by other considerations. Even if it can be shown that basic income is better placed than basic capital in mitigating stakeblowing, this may be offset by other advantages that basic capital possesses over basic income. For example, Bruce Ackerman and Anne Alstott argue that a sizeable grant has a greater capacity to transform a person's life than a basic income. Ackerman and Alstott suggest that a $80,000 stake can allow people to pay for a much wider range of life-changing events than a stream of regular but smaller payments. They comment that, 'You have a chance, once in your life, to step up to the plate. If you plan ahead, you may win big. But if you mess up, you live with the consequences. The basic income cushions failure; stakeholding is a launching pad for success' (Ackerman and Alstott 1999, 215). Proponents of a basic income might reply that an individual could try to use their projected stream of basic income to raise through borrowing a sum equivalent to a stakeholder grant. In doing this, basic income could provide access to the same opportunities as basic capital. The success of this strategy, however, depends on the ease with which a basic income could be used to raise further capital. Various imperfections in capital markets may exist which constrain the capacity of individuals to raise credit. For example, lenders may find it difficult to distinguish between those people who are likely to default on a loan and those people who will pay the loan back promptly. This information problem means that lenders may limit the availability of credit (Stiglitz and Weiss 1981). This credit rationing means that it might not be easy for a person to access a sum of money equivalent to a capital grant.

Carole Pateman's critique engenders different responses from different models of assets. Bruce Ackerman and Anne Alstott share Pateman's concern to uncouple citizenship from the workplace. They say that, 'it is time to move on to a more progressive and more inclusive system. What is required is a new master metaphor to displace the insurance analogy – and to symbolize the transition from worker citizenship to universal economic citizenship. Stakeholding provides this metaphor' (Ackerman and Alstott 1999, 15–16). Some of the policies that Ackerman and Alstott support to achieve this aim overlaps with those set out by Carol Pateman. In particular, their citizen's pension is a type of basic income scheme. Bruce Ackerman, Anne Alstott and Carol Pateman all agree about uncoupling citizenship from the workplace, but disagree about the best way to achieve this. Ackerman and Alstott prefer a basic capital and Pateman relies on a basic income.

The civic republican model marks a greater departure from Pateman's assumptions. Stuart White emphasises a principle of reciprocity that connects the receipt of material resources to a duty to act in particular ways. His version of capital grants is connected to an obligation to start a business, pay for training and put a deposit on a house. White rejects an unconditional basic income because it violates a principle of reciprocity. This emphasis on obligations diverges from the unconditional nature of Carol Pateman's proposal. The stress on obligation does not, however, be understood in terms of employment. Although one can tie basic capital or income to duties in the workplace, it is also possible to develop obligations that are unrelated to paid employment. People could be required to engage in voluntary activity in the community. Although the emphasis on obligation provides a philosophical gap between Stuart White and Carol Pateman, the fact that obligation need not be tied to employment means it is possible to create versions of capital grants that avoid the specific concern with employment.

Conclusion

This chapter has considered the assets agenda within the realm of citizenship. It has identified two important strands within models of citizenship, namely a liberal current that emphasises the importance of rights to asset-ownership and a civic republican version that combines the stress on rights with a greater injunction for people to act or behave in particular ways. I have explored the differences that exist between these strands over whether or not restrictions are imposed on how assets are used and the stress both placed on wealth taxes as a source of funding for assets. I have considered some criticisms levelled at capital grants as well as comparing basic capital with an alternative policy of providing people with a basic income.

4
Policy Options

Introduction

The previous two chapters have examined the two main traditions feeding into the assets agenda today. Chapter 2 dealt with social policy and Chapter 3 studied citizenship. This chapter rounds off this examination by highlighting some of the main themes to emerge from this discussion. I identify key differences that exist between the social policy and citizenship wings, and use a discussion of the different ways it is possible to shape the British government's Child Trust Fund scheme to provide a concrete illustration of what these differences mean in practical policy terms. Following this, I indicate that I favour a hybrid stance that combines social policy and citizenship elements when developing policy options, and I outline the core features of this hybrid approach.

The examination of the background to the assets agenda suggests that there is considerable variety in the way that asset policies may be designed. Consequently, it seems more accurate to refer to the presence of different asset agendas rather than a single asset agenda. One option for developing the assets agenda would be to rely only on social policy initiatives. This would involve measures such as Individual Development Accounts, personal savings accounts, employee share-ownership and modest capital grants. For much of the 20th century social policy has tended to rely on income benefits and public services rather than assets. Michael Sherraden comments that, 'To date, social policy for the poor has been focused almost entirely on income' (Sherraden 2003, 28). Of course, this is not to suggest that there have been no efforts previously to implement asset policies in any part of the world. However, it is true that more resources have generally been dedicated to income benefits or public services than assets. The arguments advanced in the social policy wing of the assets agenda suggests there is a case for redressing this imbalance. One of the most potent arguments for assets concerns its potential to foster investment. The idea of using investment to help prevent welfare problems from arising is appealing. Although investments in skills or human capital have often been a feature of public policy, one of the attractions of providing assets is that it extends the range of investment activities to include things other than skills. Another worthwhile aspect of asset-based social policy concerns its emphasis on equality as a foundation for economic efficiency or development. Of course, there are instances in which equality and efficiency can conflict. However, these situations do not mean that equality and efficiency are locked into an inexorable trade-off. Asset-based welfare performs a useful function of high-lighting areas in which redistribution can promote economic objectives.

Within social policy, the character development strand appears preferable to the incentives approach. It is not easy to design a system of incentives that helps achieve all the desired results. Incentives can have perverse or counterproductive effects and it may be difficult to iron out all loopholes. Added to this is the problem that behaviour will often revert to type once incentives are removed. This means the desired behavioural changes can lack a robust foundation. A character development approach avoids these difficulties. However, various qualifications should be acknowledged with the character development approach. It is a more challenging strategy for social policy as it depends on a more difficult and long-term task of changing the way people think. The nature of the asset-effect is also open to debate. Early empirical studies on Individual Development Accounts provide backing for the existence of an asset-effect. However, more detailed evidence is needed before more conclusive judgements can be made. Furthermore, there needs to be more analysis of the precise components of asset-ownership that contributes to the asset-effect.

The evidence collected in the next chapter provides some support for the character development wing of the assets agenda. The study of parents' attitudes to the Child Trust Fund found that there was support for linking the Child Trust Fund to saving. This means that there was acceptance of social policy concerns. The examination of saving provided some data in support of an asset-effect insofar as the provision of an endowment was a spur to saving. The emphasis that parents placed on restrictions on how an asset could be used means that there was a belief that incentives were not enough.

A different option for the assets agenda is to concentrate only on citizenship. This would encompass policies such as a generous and substantial capital grants and sabbatical accounts (see below). The attractive features of the citizenship agenda include its attack on wealth inequality as well as efforts to implement a 'new politics of ownership'. Wealth is unequally distributed in many parts of the world, and these levels of wealth inequality hampers individual freedom and opportunity. The new politics of ownership is also an agenda worth pursuing. For much of the 20th century debates between left and right have often focused on the merits of private property versus common, especially, state ownership. Of course, the situation was more complex than this because arguments about private versus state ownership co-existed with efforts to open up different fronts in debates about ownership. For example, Andrew Shonfield (1965) examined different forms of private property when he analysed different models of capitalism, contrasting the alleged superiority of planning in France with the unplanned capitalism in Britain. However, such efforts were overshadowed by the larger emphasis on private versus state ownership. The new politics of ownership attempts to escape the traditional dichotomy and highlight the richer and more complex forms that property may take. The assets agenda forms a component of this by studying the question of how far ownership is spread throughout society and economy.

The civic republican wing appears preferable to theories of just distribution because of the emphasis the former places on reciprocity or a duty to participate in the public realm. Stuart White makes a persuasive case for the importance of reciprocity at a conceptual level. Furthermore, reciprocity is a principle that receives empirical support. The discussions held on the Child Trust Fund, as well as earlier work that Andrew Gamble and I conducted on the attitudes of young people towards capital grants (Gamble and Prabhakar 2006), indicates that restrictions is an idea with popular appeal.

Differences between social policy and citizenship

The social policy and citizenship approaches have different implications for public administration. Cécile Fabre (2003) provides an
instance of this in her criticisms of Individual Development Accounts.
Fabre criticises Michael Sherraden's proposal to let account holders
bequeath their IDAs to their children and grandchildren. She says
that this offends against equality because it introduces a brute luck
inequality. Offspring who receive an IDA benefit from the luck of
having a parent who has saved and decided to pass on their wealth to
them. Fabre argues that liberals are also likely to reject this feature
of IDAs. For liberals the problem is that only allowing IDAs to be given
to family members constitutes an unjustified restriction on a person's
freedom to give to people outside of their family circle.

Fabre's criticisms point in opposing directions. She suggests that
liberals want to be able to bequeath to a wider range of people,
while egalitarian questions the justice of bequests. Fabre suggests a
way of mediating between these different positions. Applying the
idea that inequalities rooted in choice rather than brute luck are
fair, she says that if people are able to choose whether or not to
enter into relationships in which bequests are likely to be a feature
of those relationships, then bequests that arise from this may be
regarded as fair. While this criterion would allow bequests to family
members – where individuals choose to develop such relationships
with their family – it would not restrict bequests to family circles.

Fabre's criticisms are indicative of more general differences
between citizenship and social policy. A number of differences can
be identified in these different strands. First, the different wings
have different policy objectives. The varying aims impact upon the
way that asset policies should be judged. The social policy wing
aims to promote economic and social development. If asset policies
fail to achieve this objective, or if there are alternative policies that
are better placed to foster economic and social development, then
the case for asset policies is undermined. The citizenship strand does
not base its arguments on the contributions assets make to economic and social development, but rather views the ownership of
assets as a good thing even if it does little or nothing to support
such development.

Second, differences exist in the types of assets associated with the
different strands. The purpose of asset policies helps shape the

nature of individual policies. The different purposes associated with social policy and citizenship mean that different types of asset are linked to these strands. For example, one aim of an assets policy might be to increase the stock of savings amongst the population. An emphasis on saving sits more readily within social policy rather than citizenship. Saving fits a strategy of preventative welfare. For example, saving for retirement can help avoid pensioner poverty. Liberal models focus on the just distribution of resources, and so encouraging people to save tends to go beyond this remit. Civic republican versions of assets might have a role for saving insofar as responsibility might include a duty to save for one's future. However, one would expect civic republicans to emphasise a range of activities besides saving. Those activities that are more directly connected to the common good or public realm are likely to feature much more prominently than saving. Policies designed to foster saving, such as lifetime savings accounts, are more a feature of the social policy than citizenship.

Third, asset policies common to both the social policy and citizenship wings often differ in nature. Although social policy and citizenship have different types of assets, they also have some assets in common. For example, capital grant proposals are a feature of social policy and citizenship. Social policy research suggests that grants of around several hundred pounds are sufficient to generate an asset-effect (Bynner 2001). The citizenship wing in contrast endorses a much more substantial grant to provide people with a fair share of resources (Ackerman and Alstott 1999). Similarly, although both social policy and civic republican models can imply restrictions on how assets are used, social policy models links restrictions to economic development whereas civic republicanism allows people to pursue activities that may yield little or no economic benefit, such as volunteering in the community.

Fourth, the scope of asset policies differs between the social policy and citizenship strands. Models of citizenship concern the rights and responsibilities of all members of a political community. This means that citizenship is tied to universal asset policies. The social policy wing has room for both universal and targeted policies. Economic development could be served by allowing everyone to be in a position to make investments. Universal policies could therefore be part of a social policy approach. However, in certain circumstances economic development might be best served by concentrating limited resources on specific sections of the population. This means that social policy allows a role for targeted as well as universal schemes.

Fifth, the different wings of the assets agenda rely on different streams of funding. As noted above, there is an intimate connection between wealth taxes and the funding of assets. Social policy approaches tend to adopt a more flexible and pragmatic attitude towards funding. While this can involve wealth taxes, social policy models also allow a role for diverting money from public spending elsewhere or from funding through general taxation.

Sixth, assets are embedded in a different context within social policy and citizenship traditions. Social policy versions are part of a refashioning of the welfare state. This need not imply that assets are viewed as a replacement for traditional forms of welfare intervention such as income benefits or public services. The citizenship strand goes beyond debates about the state and engages with a broader project of creating a new politics of ownership (Pearce, Paxton and White 2006).

Example: the Child Trust Fund

The Child Trust Fund can be used to illustrate how asset policies can be developed in different ways. Early conceptions of the Child Trust Fund contained important commitments to citizenship. Gavin Kelly and Rachel Lissauer (2000) provided a forerunner to the CTF in a pamphlet entitled *Ownership for All* published by the centre-left think-tank the Institute for Public Policy Research. Kelly and Lissauer comment that a, 'centre-left strategy on asset-building should be about encouraging social inclusion and a sense of common citizenship across all individuals, regardless of income' (Kelly and Lissauer 2000, 25). Kelly and Lissauer argue that the left needs to develop a new politics of ownership, and this should involve developing models of private property that advance the goals of reformists. They say that private ownership can be used to support core left goals of opportunity, equality, autonomy and responsibility. Kelly and Lissauer say that a Children's Opportunity Fund could form one of the policies designed to create an egalitarian market economy. This policy would provide a £1,000 endowment to all new babies that would be paid into a special account that would mature once the child has grown up. Savings into this account would attract matching funds from government, and matches could be implemented on a progressive basis with children from poorer families qualifying for higher matches. The fund is intended to support individual opportunity, and Kelly and Lissauer propose that this asset be used for learning, home-ownership or entrepreneurship. David Blunkett, in his time as Secretary of State for Education and Employment, saw the CTF as a policy for supporting an active citizenry. Blunkett is concerned with tackling a malaise he detects in modern democratic politics in Britain. He points to declining turnouts at recent elections, especially among the young, and argues that the hollowing out of democracy is a problem because this undermines the legitimacy of the political system. To renew democracy he emphasises the active involvement of citizens in the political realm. He argues that owning assets helps create the conditions needed for an active and republican citizenry. He says that for, 'civic republicans' active self-government means that each citizen should have at his or her disposal the wherewithal to lead an independent life. Dependency robs the citizen of freedom. Each citizen should have an asset base so that he or she is not reduced to a state of dependence on others, and can participate fully in the life of the democracy' (Blunkett 2001, 35–36). Blunkett argues that this commitment to assets helps outline the significance of the government's proposals for a Child Trust Fund.

The above highlights a connection made between citizenship and the Child Trust Fund. This is perhaps clearest in David Blunkett's emphasis on the Child Trust Fund as a way of encouraging an active and republican citizenry. Gavin Kelly's and Rachel Lissauer's Children's Opportunity Fund is more of a hybrid, that combines measures to provide all young people with a fund that enhances individual opportunity with an element of saving. As the CTF developed in government, this policy became essentially about promoting a savings habit among the young. Her Majesty's Treasury became the lead department in developing this policy and presented this as part of a set of policies aimed at creating a savings culture. In detailed proposals on the Child Trust Fund, the Treasury notes that the, 'CTF is a vital element in the Government savings strategy which aims to ensure that a range of savings products is available to suit people at all stages in their lives' (Her Majesty's Treasury 2003,

1). The titles of the consultation documents *Savings and Assets for All* (Her Majesty's Treasury 2001a) and *Delivering Assets and Saving* (Her Majesty's Treasury 2001b) highlights the connection between assets and savings. Various explanations can be offered as to why the CTF became skewed towards savings. For example, the Treasury is more likely to be comfortable with an objective it could measure rather than a more nebulous aim of fostering a free and equal citizenship. From the perspective of this paper, what is important is that the CTF did not have to develop in this way. It could be moulded to give greater emphasis to citizenship. This alternative path underpins Alan Finlayson's (forthcoming) criticisms of the CTF as a lost opportunity to create a citizen's stake.

What would a more citizenship oriented policy look like? First, there would be a larger initial endowment. The current size of the endowment is in line with the sort of sums that are deemed necessary to generate an asset-effect. Using this policy to enhance citizenship would require the present £250 or £500 payments to be increased substantially. Bruce Ackerman comments that, 'I have nothing but praise for Tony Blair's promise to provide a small capital grant to the next generation of Britons. But a few thousand pounds in Baby Bonds is pretty small change compared to $80,000 *now*' (Ackerman 2003, 171). Of course, it seems unrealistic to expect the government to increase the endowment to an amount equivalent to a $80,000 stake given the constraints on government budgets and a plethora of other claims on spending. Nevertheless, citizenship requires a much larger initial stake. Second, the way the policy is presented is likely to differ. Dominic Maxwell and Sonia Sodha (2006) argue that the way that policies are presented or 'framed' helps embed the values associated with the policy. They say that Gavin Kelly's and Rachel Lissauer's suggestion to call this capital grant a Children's Opportunity Fund would have captured the citizenship aspirations of this policy. Maxwell and Sodha say that the Child Trust Fund is devoid of these connotations, but that it is now too late to rename this policy. They say that the labels for future developments should convey a commitment to citizenship. For example, they argue that additional top-up payments from government into these accounts at age seven should be named a 'citizen's payment'. Third, steps would be taken to counter inegalitarian aspects of present policy. Dominic Maxwell and Sonia

Sodha note that children from poorer families are less likely to be in a position to save than those from wealthy backgrounds. They suggest that different capacities of saving mean that the CTF could worsen asset inequality. To rectify this, they propose that government should consider how progressive top-ups could be placed into CTF accounts by public and private agencies. Fourth, a civic republican version would emphasise a range of other activities besides saving. Nick Pearce, Will Paxton and Stuart White (2006) say that the CTF should be used to encourage civic participation. They say that government could provide credits into CTF accounts if parents or children undertake voluntary activities in the local community, for example by acting as a governor of a local school or participating within a tenants' association. Fifth, a more generous CTF is likely to be funded by some form of wealth tax. Models of citizenship emphasise using wealth taxes as a way of paying for assets. Will Paxton, Stuart White and Dominic Maxwell (2006) edit a collection that considers how different wealth taxes (such as a land tax or inheritance tax) might be used to pay for an enhanced CTF.

A hybrid system

The different strands of the assets agenda are not mutually exclusive. It is possible to have a policy stance that contains elements of citizenship and social policy. Although different parts of the assets agenda can conflict, this does not mean that all attempts at combination are doomed to failure. A key rationale for a hybrid approach is to try and capture the advantages associated within each of the citizenship and social policy wings. This is the approach I favour. One is not forced to choose between a citizenship and social policy approach.

Hybrid approaches can be shaped in a number of ways, adding to the myriad of ways it is possible to mould the assets agenda. My preferred option would be for an approach that combines aspects of civic republican and character development approaches. Civic republicanism and character development have a shared commitment to the development of individual personality, and as such as natural partners. As noted above, the main difference between these strands is that character development stresses those activities that support economic and social development, whereas civic republicanism endorses a broader range of activities that advances the public good.

This hybrid system would involve a number of core features. First, there should be a strong commitment to universal policies. The stress on civic republicanism implies support for universal rather than targeted policies. This is echoed from a social policy perspective. The study of the Child Trust Fund conducted in Chapter 4 indicated strong parental support for universal policies. Those policies that are made available to all chimed with this opinion, and adds weight to progressive models that provide ownership for all.

Second, there is a case for a well-funded system of policies. The initial endowment of the Child Trust Fund deserves to be increased so that it could embody a statement of citizenship. At minimum, this could be in line with the £1,000 proposal set out by Gavin Kelly and Rachael Lissauer in their model of a Children's Opportunity Fund. Such an increase does not mean that all elements of saving have to be dispensed with, as increasing the stock of savings will probably boost well-being. Furthermore, the focus groups on the Child Trust Fund indicated that most parents liked having some savings element as an aspect of policy. The nature of the progressive endowment is more complex. There was disquiet about these additional payments, although this should be qualified by the lack of concern parents displayed when asking about the possibility that different children within the family might receive different endowments. Alternative tools for achieving progressive top-ups might be considered such as Kelly's and Lissauer's original suggestion of having some form of matched savings element for low-income individuals. One could alternatively opt for a much higher grant, and this would also be reasonable, although this may erode any savings element as a higher endowment could provide a disincentive to save. Julian Le Grand's and David Nissan's £10,000 scheme is likely to be the largest grant that will countenance public support.

Third, there should be a system of education in place that aids individual development. The focus groups with parents as well as an earlier empirical study of the attitudes of young people to capital grants revealed there was strong support for a policy of imposing restrictions on how assets are used. However, a policy of full blown restrictions is probably unrealistic. Following Will Paxton and Stuart White (2006), there is an argument for using a 'softer' policy of education to support responsible use. Of course, this is not an easy matter, particularly in light of the concerns parents expressed about the complexity of financial information. This raises broader issues of financial literacy and capability, and is worthy of a research project in its own right.

Fourth, there should be a mix of income, asset and public service policies. It is possible that asset policies could be conceived as a replacement for income benefits and public services, with the extension of asset policies being used to roll back income benefits or public services. Such a stance would be undesirable. The theoretical analysis suggested that income benefits and public services are likely to be important for helping assets to work and are valuable in the event that assets fail. Furthermore, there is also an issue about whether assets are always the best way of achieving various policy objectives. In certain circumstances, income benefits or public services are likely to be better policy tools for achieving specific objectives. The evidence from the focus groups on the Child Trust Fund and wealth taxation indicated that while people liked the idea of an assets policy, they wanted to see it alongside income benefits and public services. There was support for a mixed policy approach. Of course, this leaves open the question of the precise nature of the mix between income benefits and public services. The answer to this will depend on the particular policy area in question, and the character of the mix may alter over time. The key point is the need to use assets to complement other forms of public provision.

Fifth, care should be taken about how policies are presented or 'framed'. The focus groups held on attitudes to wealth taxation indicated that people's views altered depending on how policies are presented. The use of appropriately shaped stories could soften public opposition to wealth taxation. This intersects with a broader point about the 'framing' of public policy. George Lakoff (2004) argues that people rely on a web of beliefs or worldview to see the world. This provides a common sense set of assumptions that people interpret the world, and individuals respond positively to those policies that fit their worldview. He argues that the way policy is presented or 'framed' can evoke and shape particular worldviews. He says that winning public support involves framing policies in such a way that evokes particular worldviews. Policies would then chime with what people regard as common sense. He writes that, 'Framing is about getting language that fits your worldview. It is not just language. The ideas are primary – and the language carries those ideas, evokes those ideas' (Lakoff 2004, 4). Lakoff argues that language is important for evoking frames, and values should help shape the choice of language. The focus groups on wealth taxation suggests that although Lakoff's thesis can be overstated, in that stories designed to increase support for inheritance tax had limited success, it is nevertheless the case that framing seemed to have an impact. Debates about assets should be couched explicitly in terms of values, and it appears that this could help increase public support for asset policies.

Sixth, attention should be paid to developing a community fund scheme to help pay for an expanded assets programme. Although the case for using a wealth tax to pay for assets is strong at a theoretical level, the evidence from focus groups suggests that difficulties are likely to be encountered in relying on this to pay for assets. While this does not rule out the use of wealth taxes, nor suggests that support for wealth taxes cannot be enhanced, the evidence presented here suggests that a community fund should be a line of policy development. Arguments would have to be made though about using the proceeds of a community fund to pay for assets, and this connects with the need to provide an attractive framing of policy.

Conclusion

This chapter completes the first task of this book, that is an examination of the intellectual background to the assets agenda. I now proceed from theory to evidence, by presenting in the next two chapters original evidence relating to the provision and funding of assets.

5
The Child Trust Fund

Introduction

This chapter moves this book from theory to evidence. The previous two chapters explored the theoretical background to assets within social policy and citizenship. This chapter and the next reports original evidence conducted on the assets agenda, looking respectively at general issues of provision and funding.

In this chapter I focus on the Child Trust Fund. The opening chapter signalled the importance of studying this particular initiative, both because of the international interest in this policy and because it is a concrete example of a universal asset policy. The study of the Child Trust Fund touches upon the broader topic of the provision of assets, as it considers the different forms that assets may take.

This chapter considers the views of parents. Parents are crucial to the success of the Child Trust Fund for several reasons. First, parents are supposed to open an account in their child's name. They have to choose among the three main types of accounts on offer, namely an interest-bearing cash account, a stakeholder account or a non-stakeholder shares account (the latter two invest funds on the stock market). Only if parents do not open an account within the first year of receiving the Child Trust Fund does Her Majesty's Revenue and Customs (HMRC) step in and open a stakeholder account for the child. Second, parents will make many of the key decisions about saving once the account is opened. Parents will decide how much to save, particularly during the early years of their child's life. Third, as the child gets older parents will probably play an important role in guiding children how to use their accounts.

Initial indications suggest, however, that this policy is not working as well as it might. According to the official figures, of the 2.56 million Child Trust Fund vouchers issued by June 2006, 1.81 million accounts had been opened by the end of this period. This means that around 750,000 accounts have not been opened, which is around 30 per cent of total vouchers issued. A quarter of the earliest Child Trust Fund vouchers (issued between January and March 2005) have been unopened by parents (http://www.hmrc.gov.uk/stats/child_trust_funds/ctf-sept06.pdf). Of course, policies often take time to bed down, and one would expect the proportion of unopened accounts to fall as time progresses. However, even allowing for this the portion of unopened accounts seems significant. This has led some commentators to question whether parents value this policy. In January 2006 Carl Emmerson, deputy director of the Institute for Fiscal Studies, stated that it is not clear whether the unopened accounts signal that parents are simply taking their time to choose among the different accounts or, more worryingly, that parents are failing to engage with this policy (news.bbc.co.uk/1/hi/business/4620154.stm, accessed 20/2/2006).

Little is known, however, about what parents think of this policy. This chapter adds to our current evidence base by presenting evidence derived from focus groups on the reaction of parents towards the Child Trust Fund. The aim is to learn from experience and derive information useful for the development of this policy. The evidence presented here is from a small-scale qualitative study and so care has to be taken not to exaggerate the impact of these results. Nevertheless, the focus groups did provide a broad indication of what parents think of this policy.

Focus groups

Focus groups were used in this study. Focus groups are a familiar tool of social research (Kreuger 1994; Morgan 1997; Bloor, Frankland, Thomas and Robson 2001). They have been used in several studies related to assets research. These have been used to generate stand-alone findings as well as combined with other research methods (Commission on Taxation and Citizenship 2000; Edwards 2000, 2001; Rowlingson and McKay 2005). Focus groups were selected for this study for two main reasons. First, as a tool for exploration. Focus groups allow participants an opportunity to shape the issues being studied as well as the options under discussion. This is valuable for research that may not know at the outset all the issues that matter (Morgan 1997). The importance of this is confirmed by that fact that a substantial proportion of parents have left their Child Trust Fund unopened. This suggests that the policy has left some of the key concerns of parents unaddressed. Second, focus groups allow for group deliberation or interaction (Morgan 1997). This group interaction can provide clues as to what options for design are likely to command public assent. This is useful for helping to determine which versions of the Child Trust Fund, if any, are likely to garner public support.

The evidence in this chapter comes from seven focus groups in England convened in January and February 2006. About eight parents attended each group, with 58 participants in all. The study covered parents who receive the standard £250 voucher as well as those who qualify for the higher £500 payment. About a third of participants had the higher £500 payment. Although the bulk of participants were female, a function of the fact that parents' groups are dominated by mothers, several men took part in the study. Individuals were each paid a £20 incentive payment for taking part in the discussion. The discussions lasted about one hour. At the end of the session, participants filled in a brief sheet setting out some basic details about their account (asking for example, whether they had added to the account).

Sites were based in both northern and southern England and covered both urban and rural locations. Three groups were held in Cambridgeshire, three in Derbyshire and one in London. One pilot was also held in London in December 2005 although data from this pilot is not used in the results here. The parents groups were all based at Sure Start centres. These centres are based in deprived areas of the country and provide facilities and activities for families with young children living within the area. Sure Start centres were selected for several reasons. First, they offered a way of accessing parents from low-income households. Parents from low-income households were often reluctant to identify themselves because they felt a stigma was attached to belonging to such households. By being based in deprived areas, Sure Start offered a way of accessing parents who qualify for the £500 payment without too much intrusion. Second, the centres helped isolate the impact of household income on reactions to the Child Trust Fund (household income is used to decide the different Child Trust Fund payments). Sure Start centres are open to all who live in a neighbourhood, and this includes the affluent and non-affluent. These centres allowed an insight into the views of higher-income parents who share much of the same environment as low-income parents. This helped reduce the possibility of other factors (such as living in an area with better public services) coming into play between low and high-income households. The groups that were convened drew in people from a wide range of income backgrounds. Third, the centres possess facilities supportive of discussion groups (such as meeting rooms, on-site crèches). In addition, as most of the participants already attend groups at the centres, they provide a familiar and welcoming environment for parents. Letters were sent out to the directors of the Sure Start centres detailing the nature of the project and the desired content of the groups. Sure Start staff then recruited the members of the groups.

The study of the Child Trust Fund draws upon the previous theoretical exploration. The scrutiny of the Child Trust Fund is organised around two main themes. First, an examination of attitudes towards the policy as it currently stands. Second, a discussion of alternatives to the present policy. Each of these themes is informed by the analysis of social policy and citizenship. For example, part of the study of the policy as it currently stands concentrates on the asset-effect hypothesis found within social policy. Similarly, the discussion of policy alternatives addresses the social policy concern that the public funds dedicated to the Child Trust Fund would be better spent on other types of social policy. The discussion of alternatives also considers a key disagreement within models of citizenship, that is whether or not restrictions ought to be imposed on how assets are used. While it is not possible to explore all the theoretical issues of interest, evidence is nevertheless collected on some key issues.

What do parents think about the present version of the Child Trust Fund?

Size

One of the key differences between a citizenship and social policy version of capital grants relates to the size of the capital endowment. Social policy analysis suggests that a grant of several hundred pounds is sufficient to generate an asset-effect, whereas citizenship endorses a much larger grant. The modest size of the Child Trust

Fund is closer to models of social policy than citizenship. The questions asked about capital grants picked up this difference between social policy and citizenship.

Parents were initially asked about what they thought of the current size of the Child Trust Fund. Did parents think of the grant as merely a token or gimmick?

Most of the parents were happy with the size of the initial endowments, feeling them to be about right. The prevailing view also seemed to be that it would be churlish to complain as it is a gift from government.

- *Parent, £500, Derbyshire*
  250 is a nice little starter and 500 you can't complain can you really.
- *Parent, £250, Cambridgeshire*
  I think it's better than nothing. It's a lot more than what people got in the past.

Questions were raised from within the groups about what the grants would be worth in 18 years if there were no additional payments from any source. Using figures from the government, it was explained that if the grants were placed in a normal interest account with no further payments from any source, then the grants would roughly double (so £250 would be worth around £500, and £500 roughly £1,000). Most parents felt that these figures would not be worth much in 18 years time. Two themes emerged from this particular discussion. First, parents typically emphasised the importance of adding to the accounts over the 18 years in order to increase its value. Second, the broadly positive attitudes towards the initial endowments did not diminish with the knowledge of what it could be worth in 18 years if left untouched. Most felt that something was still better than nothing.

- *Parent, £500, Cambridgeshire*
  Say for some sad reason I stay on income support for the next 18 years, I'm still not going to have £250 I'm going to be able to give on my child's 18th birthday for a present. And the government is going to give her 500 and that's got to be better than nothing.

To examine attitudes towards a more citizenship oriented policy, parents were asked about their attitudes towards a substantial increase in the size of the initial endowment. People were asked about increasing the Child Trust Fund to a £10,000 grant. Julian Le Grand's and David Nissan's (2000) demogrant proposal was used to shape this particular option. Opinions were divided about this idea. Many parents reacted positively to this proposal. These parents thought a £10,000 grant would significantly enhance their child's opportunities.

- *Parent, £250, Cambridgeshire*
  To be perfectly honest, given the choice between the two, I would prefer to have the £10,000 and have those three restrictions than the £250, £500 that we've all got because like I say I've had feelings about why this has come about, lets not dress it up as something it isn't. Let's just say what it is. It's money for education, to start your own business or to get you on the first rung of the housing ladder. It makes far more sense.

Balanced against this, however, were concerns about the costs of such a programme. A substantial proportion of parents felt it was not realistic financially to provide a £10,000 grant. Added to this were worries about misusing or 'blowing' such a substantial sum of money. Thus, while a move towards a more citizenship oriented policy did engender public support, this was qualified by concerns about cost and responsible use.

Progressive universalism

The Child Trust Fund provides an example of 'progressive universalism'. The payment of £250 to all new babies marks the universal part of the Child Trust Fund, while the additional £250 payment is the progressive element. There was a mixed reaction to this structure. There was strong support for the payment of a grant to all new babies. Most parents felt that if it should go to one baby, then it should go to all babies. Some parent did question, however, whether children from very rich backgrounds should get it. The prevailing attitude, however, is that all should get it. The sentiment was that it was not fair to a child to deny them a grant simply because of their parents' circumstances. Policy should treat children independently of parental background. The strong commitment to universalism suggests a lack of support for those models of social policy that rely on targeted schemes.

This emphasis on treating children separately from parents fuelled a concern with the progressive element of the Child Trust Fund. Most parents were against a two-tier payment and were in favour instead of a single flat-rate grant. This view was shared by parents who received the £500 as well as £250 payments. Although recipients of the £500 grant were happy with the extra amount, they felt that everyone should get the same.

- *Parent, £500, Cambridgeshire*
I think everyone is the same at the end of the day, people like me who are on income support, why should I get £500? I know it's my child but at the end of the day just because I'm on a lower income shouldn't mean I should get more money. I think everyone should be treated the same.
- *Parent, £500, Derbyshire*
If you work you'll only get £250. Whereas I don't work and so we'd be entitled to £500. But why deny someone who's working?

The emphasis parents placed on treating children separately from the parents meant that they tended to think that the financial circumstances of the household should not be taken into account when deciding on the grant. In addition, attention was drawn to the way that household income might change over time, so a rich family could be poor in 18 years time and vice versa. Parents thought that the best way of dealing with these household dynamics is simply to make a single flat-rate grant.

Sibling rivalry

Some commentators believe that the progressive structure of the Child Trust Fund is unfair. Carl Emmerson and Matthew Wakefield (2001) argue that the progressive structure creates the possibility that children within the same family might receive different endowments from government. In particular, household income might change so that while one child qualifies for a £250 voucher, a brother or sister might be entitled to a higher £500 payment. Emmerson and Wakefield argue that the provision of different grants highlights an intrinsic unfairness with the Child Trust Fund.

Worries about siblings were a particular concern of parents. This issue was raised by parents themselves in virtually all of the groups.

Alongside concerns about information, this issue constituted the principal source of parental dissatisfaction with the Child Trust Fund. The issue was not, however, about children receiving different amounts but rather about those children who did receive a Child Trust Fund and those brothers and sisters who did not. Parents emphasised treating their children equally. Generally speaking, they did not regard the possibility of different children getting different amounts as particularly problematic. They thought that a child who received the £250 payment would also benefit from a higher household income, and so parents could be better able to save than in circumstances in which a child receives £500.

- *Parent, £250, Cambridgeshire*
I don't think different amounts are a problem, I just think one getting it and one not is going to cause fights when they're older.
- *Parent, £500, Derbyshire*
They've all had a starter whether it's 250 or 500, but if parents could make sure when they turn 18 they both get the same amount.

This lack of concern with siblings getting different endowments contrasted with the general criticisms parents levelled at the progressive element of the Child Trust Fund. People seemed more willing to accept different endowments within their own family over different endowments provided to children from different families. This highlights that the responses that parents made were not always consistent.

Most of the groups had parents with children born before the September 2002 cut-off date for the Child Trust Fund in addition to a child or children who received the grant. They felt that the policy was unfair to those siblings born before the September 2002 cut-off.

- *Parent, £500, Derbyshire*
I've got three children who didn't get it and I got two that did. The first three didn't get it, so for them that aren't going to get it when they're older, to have money given, well that'll be unfair ... my eldest three are going to think, well when they're 18 they've got such and such, what have we got? We can't afford to save because we're only on benefits. Five children, so like when my eldest one turns 18, and he [points to baby] turns 18, he's got £1000, what have I got, where's mine?

- *Parent, £250, Cambridgeshire*
I don't think it's fair. I've got a 7 year old that doesn't get it and I've got two children who do get it. I haven't opened an account for her yet because I can't afford to, but in a few years time when their money comes in, she's going to feel her brother and sister have got money in the bank but she hasn't because I haven't personally been able to put any money in.

Although parents understood the view that policy had to start somewhere, and that this problem would erode in the future, there was still a view that the policy was unfair to brothers and sisters born before September 2002.

Parents with children who had some children who had the Child Trust Fund and others that did not took various steps to correct this perceived unfairness. Most reported they would save for the children without the grant first before putting money into the Child Trust Fund. This situation was more difficult, however, for parents with children on the £500 payment as they reported more difficulties in saving.

- *Parent, £500, Cambridgeshire*
What I did was actually drill off the money off a credit card believe it or not, so that both of them had accounts together ... they've got to both be equal. When my daughter hits 18 she needs to have the same as what the other one will get.

When asked what government could do for children who did not get the grant, most parents said that the government should provide grants for the other children that do not currently receive it. When parents were asked whether all other children up to age 18 should be able to qualify for a Child Trust Fund (to cover situations where parents have teenagers up to the age 18 as well as a new baby), parents felt that if older children were still at school then they should get a Child Trust Fund. Another alternative suggested by parents themselves was to allow them to divide up the Child Trust Fund between children who do and do not receive the grant.

Locked nature of grants

Most parents supported the fact that money in the Child Trust Fund is locked away for a substantial period of time. Parents felt that the locked nature would help them save for their child. They stated that if the account could be accessed at any time, then it was likely that the money would be spent on various expenses as they crop up. In some cases, parents said the locked nature seemed to encourage family and friends to add to the account because they knew the money was going to the child.

- *Parent, £500, Cambridgeshire*
  I think that's good because it's so easy for children or parents just to dip into it. I think it's good that it stays there for 18 years, they can't touch it, but I think in 18 years that the child shouldn't be able to touch it either, that they should get guidance.
- *Parent, £250, London*
  One person gave us money for her that they wouldn't have given us. They didn't give it to any of the other grandchildren and they probably wouldn't have given it to us if we all could get our hands on it.

Parents felt that the accounts should if anything have a longer life-span. Most were happier if the account could mature when the child was in their early 20s rather than 18 as they thought that children would be more likely to use it wisely at 21 than 18.

Saving

Too much information

Questions were asked about saving was used to examine the 'asset-effect'. Michael Sherraden (1991) highlights the asset-effect has a number of components. There was not time to explore all of these facets in these focus groups. Instead, questions concentrated on savings. This was because savings is probably the key policy priority of the Child Trust Fund.

The groups started off by questioning those who had not opened an account. The majority of focus groups had parents who had not opened accounts, and in these groups around one quarter of parents had not opened their child's accounts. The evidence from the focus groups suggests that parents are not failing to engage with the policy.

When asked about their overall reaction to this policy, most parents responded in a positive fashion, saying that they believe it is a good idea and support it in principle.

- *Parent, £500, Derbyshire*
  It's basically a good idea, it needs fine tuning I think, but it's a good idea.
- *Parent, £250, Cambridgeshire*
  I think it's a good idea, but I think more information should be readily available.

Those parents who failed to open accounts say that the main reason for this is to do with the information associated with the policy. On the one hand, there were complaints about too much information. Many parents reported being overwhelmed with leaflets and fliers from financial bodies.

- *Parent, £250, London*
  I think there's too much. I've picked leaflets, and fliers, and key features and things, from Lloyd's bank, and from Abbey National, all that sort of thing. And they provide too much waffle and not enough key features. They don't tell who is actually running the fund? Is it Deutsche fund managers running it? Or, if I want to find out how the fund is doing, where do I find out where the fund is? What's it in? And at the end of the day, when they're 18 I know that if it's £250 and you don't add to it it's not going to be that much, even in a unit trust. But you want the best out of it, and I don't think there's what I call a bells and whistle guide to the different funds.
- *Parent, £250, Derbyshire*
  You just got that much information you don't know where to start.

Parents said that the first year of their baby's life was a demanding time for them, and they did not have the time or energy to sift properly through the information they received. On the other hand, concerns were expressed about the quality of the information that was available. It was reported that information was often confusing and incomplete.

- *Parent, £500, Cambridgeshire*
  Well, me I don't personally know much about stakeholder, this that and the other. You can read and read and read and read, and it doesn't

really make much sense, especially to a single mum, blah blah blah, I've been given a cheque, there you go, you've got so much time to sort it out. And you just get blinded by it all, and to me it's just a bit too complicated.

Concerns were expressed about the presence of hidden charges and lack of transparency. In some cases it was said that financial providers appeared to lack the information themselves.

- *Parent, £250, Derbyshire*
When I went to enquire at the bank they said oh it's higher up what's doing it, it's not the actual branches what are doing it ... it's customer service higher up.

When asked what sort of information parents would like, the most popular answer was for a simple and transparent fact sheet setting out key features of the policy. This would provide information on what the Child Trust Fund would be worth in 18 years if various amounts were placed in the account, what charges are associated with the account, where money for the accounts are invested, and which organisations are doing the investing. The government was seen to have a key role in the provision of such information.

- *Parent, £250, Cambridgeshire*
Probably more information on, maybe statistics on what stock markets have done over the last few years. As a parent who doesn't know much about the stock market, you can make an educated decision based upon facts that you can actually see, the rises and falls, and draw your own conclusions from everything.
- *Parent, £500, Derbyshire*
People who supply it, what they charge, the interest rate.

One option proposed by some of the parents was for government to open automatically an account for the child, and the parents could then switch this if they were unhappy with this account. There was also some support for a smaller number of providers in the market, which would make the task of choosing among the options easier. These possibilities were not, however, universally accepted. Some concern was expressed about the possibility of collusion between government and providers if there are a small set of providers, and some liked the fact that parents are responsible for choosing an account themselves. There was general agreement, however, that the current information base is not adequate and this acts as a barrier to the successful operation of this policy.

Saving

The questions then turned to those who had opened accounts to see if the provision of an account had caused them to think any differently about saving. Some reported that Child Trust Fund had made them think differently.

- *Parent, £250, London*
  I can only talk for myself. For my first one, for birthdays and Christmas he got money, he got money, he always got money for christening. And that just went. You always found something to spend it on. With her I must admit, for christening, all that money has gone into a savings account. And now, when her birthday comes I've said to the godparents, I don't want any more toys or clothes. I've given them the account and told them to do what they want. And that's it.
- *Parent, £250, Derbyshire*
  Because I'm not good at saving money but I've had that incentive to start saving for it and so I've started saving for it. Somebody's helped me out by putting an amount in an account for them, I'm not just going to leave that account. Like everyone else, £250 or £500 in 18 years is going to be nothing so I'm building on that so that the interest on that is all building up and so she is going to have something when she's older. I've never had that opportunity, I never got given so many thousands of pounds when I turned 18, or even now when I'm 21 I've never had any amount of money given to me so I want her to have an opportunity that I didn't have.

What appeared to be important were the initial funds provided by government. This seemed to help kick-start saving. Parents said that family and friends had shown interest in saving into the accounts, especially around the child's birthday or Christmas. Some parents explicitly asked that on these special occasions, family and friends place deposits into the Child Trust Fund instead of buying presents. Although there was an indication of an asset-effect among some parents, this was not true of all parents. Most of those who had opened acccounts reported that they had not yet added to the accounts. Overall, there was some, but only mild, support for an increase in saving.[1]

Of the accounts that were opened, most parents opted for an interest bearing cash account. Some parents were wary of investing in shares because of previous bad experiences with the stock markets as well as endowment mortgages. Others stated that they were not happy to take risks with their child's money. Parents recognised that share accounts have an element of risk, but felt that as the Child Trust Fund is not their money but their child's, they should not put it at risk. Parents said, however, that if the child wishes eventually to move it into a share-based account, then that would be up to the child.

- *Parent, £250, Derbyshire*
  I went for a normal savings account, at the end of the day that money's my daughter's so I just went for a normal savings account. … She can do what she wants with her money, but I didn't want to risk her money.

One concern expressed with saving within the social policy community is that low-income individuals are not in a position to save. Writing in his capacity as the director of the Child Poverty Action Group, Martin Barnes (2002) argues that low-income individuals lack the financial resources to save into assets. Although recent work suggests that low-income individuals are able to save if sufficient incentives are in place (Kempson, McKay and Collard 2005), worries about the capacity of low-income individuals to save are a persistent concern with asset-based welfare.

In the focus groups parents who received the £500 payment reported more difficulties in saving than those with the £250 voucher. The former often said that they could not afford to save much.

- *Parent, £500, Derbyshire*
  We can't afford to put any extra on a regular basis. I mean every now and then, birthday or Christmas when he gets some money. But I can't afford to do regular savings.

While it is true that parents from low-income households found it more difficult to save, they did not tend to regard the Child Trust

Fund as a middle-class policy and unfair. They tended to see different capacities to save as a fact of life and thought at least the Child
Trust Fund gave the child something.

- *Parent, £500, Derbyshire*
  *It's up to you, you know, if you want a better job and get paid more
  then get more training and get another job. It's your responsibility at
  the end of the day.*
- *Parent, £500, Cambridgeshire*
  *If you got the money to save you do, if you don't you don't, there's
  nothing you can do about it.*

To bring out a difference between social policy and citizenship,
parents were asked whether they preferred their children to have a
policy like the Child Trust Fund or simply a grant for their children
without the savings element as they reached adulthood. The latter
would simply be a mark of citizenship. While a straightforward
grant had a number of supporters, the majority of parents favoured
some sort of savings element.

What do parents think about alternatives?

Responsible use

Questions about restrictions were used mainly to provide data
on different models of citizenship. A key difference between civic
republicanism and theories of just distribution concerns whether
or not restrictions should be imposed on how assets are used.
Almost all of the parents were concerned about the possibility of
stakeblowing.

- *Parent, £500, Cambridgeshire*
  *Worried in case that, everyone knows when they're 18 they're going to
  get this money and all of a sudden they've got all good friends and
  everything. Next thing you know, they're down the pub, you know
  against the wall, and for what?*
- *Parent, £250, Derbyshire*
  *I'm not saying every 18 year old is the same, because they're not, but
  most 18 year olds, they'll say 18 grand, I know what I'm going to do
  with that, go out Saturday night, get absolutely bladdered, holiday, get*

a car and then they'll be in debt. And then they'll be thinking when they're 21, oh my god.

Parents favoured placing restrictions on how assets are used. When asked what sorts of restriction they prefer, the most common responses were spending the grant on university or buying a home. These sentiments tend to chime with civic republicanism rather than models of just distribution. A policy of restrictions, however, is not confined to civic republicanism. Character development social policy models also allow a role for restrictions. As noted above, the main difference between civic republicanism and character development is that the former allows a role for activities that yield little or no economic benefit. To explore general attitudes towards linking the Child Trust Fund to activities that do not yield any obvious economic benefit, parents were asked what they thought about their child using their grant to take a gap year and travel the world. Most parents saw this as a worthwhile expenditure as this would broaden the mind. There were, however, some dissenting voices that thought a holiday was frivolous. A follow-up question in some of the groups focused more narrowly upon civic republicanism by asking about attitudes towards providing credits into the account for the child engaging in voluntary activity in the local community. People did not tend to have strong views either way about this suggestion. There was no great clamour or opposition to this proposal. Some expressed concern though that this proposal might mean that some parents put pressure on their child to undertake voluntary activity as a way of avoiding their own responsibilities to save into the fund.

Although there was general emphasis on responsible use, there was less agreement about whether formal restrictions should be imposed on how the Child Trust Fund is used. Some felt that while parents should play an important role in guiding and educating their child to use their Child Trust Fund wisely, ultimately it should be the child's decision on what to spend their fund on. These views were consistent with the suggestion by Will Paxton and Stuart White (2006) to implement a system of targeted mentoring. Paxton and White say that while full-blown restrictions on use are probably impractical, education programmes with additional assistance for specific individuals could be used to guide people to use their stakes wisely.

- *Parent, £250, London*

If you educate them throughout their lives and you teach them how to deal with money then probably you wouldn't have such a problem with them just blowing it. Having said that, there's no guarantee, anyway, even, if you do put restrictions on it, there's no guarantee.

- *Parent, £250, Derbyshire*

I think that's where your parenting comes in, you try to influence your child to try and use that money or to save it for if they need a car to get to work or something a bit sensible. Not just to blow it on a car, but if they need a car to get from a to b, say for deposit on a mortgage, or if they need it for their university fees. I think you've got to influence the child haven't you to use it for something, not to just blow it.

Although some parents favoured general guidance, others wanted formal restrictions on grants. However, parents wanted parents rather than government to frame these restrictions.

- *Parent, £500, Cambridgeshire*

At the end of the day if the government is going to give you money and then they decide, then that's just taking my child back. It's like I'm supposed to be the parent, I'm supposed to be responsible. Nobody's given me the chance. Here's the money, you're not allowed to touch it, it's for your child but we're going to tell you how to spend it. What's the point of giving it?

- *Parent, £500, Derbyshire*

Not a free country if government starts saying that. It's your money, at the end of the day it's your child's money. No matter what you say or do, they're going to do what they're going to do with it aren't they? But you can't start saying we say you can't do this, you can't do that.

Parents wanted some form of parental control over how their child spends their funds, suggesting as one option that children should be required to get parental consent before enacting spending plans. Parents recognised that this might lead to problems for those families in which parents and children did not have a good relationship, but maintained nevertheless that parents should have some form of control.

This concern about parental control dissuaded some from saving into the Child Trust Fund. Although these parents reported that they would save for their children, they reported that they had set up and were saving in a different account over which they could exercise control. In some cases parents reported that financial advisors had advised them not to save into the Child Trust Fund but to save into a different account precisely because of this concern about parental control.

> • *Parent, £250, Cambridgeshire*
> *When we spoke to this financial adviser, he actually advised us not to put any extra money into that particular account because it was going to get locked up and because you have no control over how your child spends it. He actually advised that if you did want to make regular savings, you should open a separate account to which you do have control.*

Spending on income benefits or public services

One of the key criticisms of asset-based welfare is whether this policy represents the best use of scarce public funds (Emmerson and Wakefield 2001; Davey 2006). This fuels Liberal Democrat opposition to the Child Trust Fund which, alone among the major political parties, pledged to abolish the Child Trust Fund as part of its 2005 general election campaign. The 2005 manifesto says the promise to divert the £1.5 billion dedicated to the Child Trust Fund to spending on early years education as one of 10 good reasons to vote Liberal Democrat at the general election (Liberal Democrats 2005).

Two main alternatives were discussed in the focus groups. First, higher spending on income benefit. In particular parents were asked if they would prefer the money spent on the Child Trust Fund to be spent instead on boosting their Child Benefit, which they can access immediately and choose to spend how they wish. Initially parents were asked this question in relation to the current level of the Child Trust Fund. Thus, the option was to use the £250 or £500 endowment to boost Child Benefit. For those in receipt of the £250 payment, this meant about an extra £5 a week for their baby's first year. For those who received the £500 grant, this would amount roughly to an extra £10 a week on their Child Benefit for a year. Faced with choice, there was general agreement for the Child Trust Fund over the income supplement on Child Benefit. This covered those who received the £500 as well as £250 payments. Parents argued that their child would probably benefit more from the savings in the future than the extra income today.

- *Parent, £500, Derbyshire*
I prefer the voucher because at the end of the day my Child Benefit, it goes on things like nappies and things like that, whereas if they registered my Child Benefit it wouldn't get saved for it.
- *Parent, £250, Derbyshire*
My child's Child Benefit gets spent on her nappies, on her clothes, on her this and on her that. She's not going to see the benefit of that when she's older is she? 'Oh I've got a fiver a week extra, so mum bought me some nappies'. She's not going to think like that is she?

Parents were then asked about their views about the extra on Child Benefit if the Child Trust Fund was £1,000 for all instead of their current levels (this would mean around an extra £20 a week for the baby's first year). Again, most parents favoured the Child Trust Fund, although some parents said they would waver if the money were increased. Parents did not show an appetite, however, for Child Benefit being cut to finance a higher Child Trust Fund, preferring a mix of income and assets policies.

Second, parents were asked for their views about spending money dedicated to the Child Trust Fund on public services instead, especially pre-school and primary education. The response of most parents were in favour of the Child Trust Fund rather than extra money on public services. Parents tended to be more reluctant about spending money on public services rather than Child Benefit. A common view was that enough of peoples' taxes had already gone to pay for education.

- *Parent, £500, Derbyshire*
You pay your taxes, you pay for them, they should be getting enough by now.
- *Parent, £250, Cambridgeshire*
I'm totally against that because I think we've paid in for years to taxes that should have gone in for education anyway.

Parents were also cynical about the government's motivations for public services, believing that government would use the provision of policies such as the Child Trust Fund to justify cuts in public spending elsewhere.

> • *Parent, £500, Derbyshire*
> *What I want to know is are they going to be penalised for having money in the bank account when they leave school. That's what I think the government's going it for, so they don't have to pay as much for when they can't get a job, when they've got a family to look after or whatever. I say they're going to get penalised, saying you've got all that money in there, live on that.*

There was no support for rolling back public services, although when asked some parents were willing to countenance cuts in specific areas of public services to fund a higher Child Trust Fund. In some of the groups, some were prepared to support cuts in higher education spending to fund a higher Child Trust Fund for all.

Discussion

The focus groups suggested that most parents broadly welcomed the Child Trust Fund, although there was concern about the specifics of policy design. Some tentative themes can be identified from these discussions that are likely to be important for the future development of this policy. I do not propose definite answers to these issues, but rather signpost, things that ought to be addressed for the future.

First, greater attention should be paid to the information surrounding this policy. One of the most persistent complaints across all the groups were about a lack of adequate information about the Child Trust Fund. While most parents saw a benefit in opening a Child Trust Fund account for their children, a key reason why some people opened accounts and others didn't was related to the ease with which they could process the available information. Participants in fact had only had a partial knowledge about all the features of the Child Trust Fund at the outset of the sessions. For example, many were unaware of the two-tier payment structure, and there was also uncertainty about the maximum amounts that could be saved into the Child Trust Fund account each year. This raises challenges for providers, individuals and government. Banks and building societies have to transmit information in a simple, clear and comprehensive manner. Of course, this issue is more easily stated than achieved. No doubt, many financial institutions already make efforts to communicate with their customers in a transparent fashion. However, the evidence from the focus groups suggests that more could be done. Liaising with government agencies, financial regulators and groups representing parents could assist with this process. A challenge for government is how to regulate better the quantity and quality of the information from the financial sector. Individuals also have a role to play, as understanding material is not simply a matter of providing adequate information. People must be able to interpret and act upon this information, and this highlights the need for skills or capacities. There was evidence in the groups that parents themselves used baby groups as a way of sharing information and advice. Such local networks offer a possible avenue for developing understanding or capability.

Second, some steps ought to be taken to provide assistance to those siblings that do not receive a Child Trust Fund. Parents wanted to treat all their children equally. The provision of a Child Trust Fund to some but not all of their children was a key source of dissatisfaction. Although there was recognition that policy had to start from somewhere, there was a desire to have something for those siblings that did not have a Child Trust Fund. One solution could be to provide all older siblings with their own Child Trust Fund. A difficulty with this, however, is that this would probably substantially increase the cost of this programme. Furthermore, paying Child Trust Funds at a later date would not capitalise on the potential benefits in developing individual character that could occur by paying this at birth. Allowing parents to divide the Child Trust Fund would probably make this policy too complex to administer. Perhaps the most realistic option is to accept that this policy has to start from somewhere. However, government, banks and building societies could draw attention to the range of other accounts that are available for older children.

Third, moves should be made to address concerns over responsible use. Full-blown restrictions are probably impractical. However, parents seemed amenable to the idea of providing education and guidance, and here Will Paxton's and Stuart White's advocacy of education, supportive advice and targeted mentoring deserves further investigation. This focus can be linked to the broader issue of financial capability mentioned above.

Fourth, any further extension of asset policies should be geared towards universal policies. A key debate within social policy concerns the merits of universal versus targeted benefits. An apparently puzzling aspect of the Child Trust Fund is why a government that has often extended means-tested benefits should have implemented a universal assets policy. The reasons for this are complex, and cannot be investigated here. However, one message from the focus groups is for a preference for universal schemes, and so any further asset policies should be biased towards universal schemes.

Conclusion

This chapter has provided original evidence on parental attitudes to the Child Trust Fund. The broad picture is one of general support for this policy with concerns about specific elements of its design. The chapter has been structured around a discussion of the policy as it currently stands and an examination of policy alternatives. The distinction between social policy and citizenship informed the nature of the questions.

Much of the present version of the Child Trust Fund is shaped by a social policy agenda. For example, the current size of the Child Trust Fund is in line with social policy research rather than citizenship. The discussions held with parents indicated support for elements of a social policy agenda. Most parents were content with the current endowments and basic features of the Child Trust Fund. Respondents did not want to see the Child Trust abolished in favour of extra spending on income benefits or public services.

There is scope, however, for shaping the policy so that it incorporates more elements from a citizenship agenda. There is potential for increasing the size of the endowments to provide a more generous citizen's stake. There is also strong support for imposing restrictions on how the capital grant is used.

6
Paying for Assets

Introduction

This chapter moves the empirical discussion from the provision to the funding of assets. I consider different ways of paying for asset policies. This chapter draws on the ideas covered in Chapters 3 and 4 for paying for assets. This looks at two main sources of funding. First the use of wealth taxes. Chapter 3 noted that an emphasis on wealth taxes to pay for assets is a common thread across different models of citizenship. I examine public attitudes towards wealth taxes, looking specifically at inheritance tax and land tax. Second, alternatives to wealth taxes. This picks up on the suggestion made in social policy circles of using cuts in existing forms of public spending rather than the imposition of additional taxes as a way of raising money. The chapter also considers the proposal of using a community fund to raise extra money for assets.

The discussions reported below used the example of how to boost the Child Trust Fund to examine more general attitudes for paying for savings. Dominic Maxwell and Sonia Sodha (2006) suggest that a good deal is achieved once a policy, however modest, is implemented. In particular, asset policies require a framework of supporting policies, and that implementing asset policies lays down the necessary 'plumbing' for further measures. Once the plumbing has been laid, the taps can be turned on for the extension of asset policies. One way that the taps can be turned on for asset policies is for a more generous Child Trust Fund.

Of course, one can support the streams of funding considered in this chapter without also backing asset policies. For example, wealth taxes could be justified simply as a way of tackling wealth inequality. Edward Wolff says that, 'If one policy goal is to moderate the rising inequality of recent years, direct taxation of wealth is one proposed remedy' (Wolff 2002, 67). Edward Wolff (2001) reports wealth inequality in the United States is more unequally distributed than income and is now at a 70 year high. He says that while wealth inequality gradually fell from the 1930s to the 1970s, it increased during the 1980s and 1990s. Using data for 1998, Wolff (2001) says that the top 1 per cent of wealth holders own 38 per cent of all household wealth (that is financial wealth such as shares and bank accounts as well as non-financial wealth such as housing) while the top 20 per cent own 83 per cent of household wealth. Concentrating more narrowly on financial wealth, he notes that the richest 1 per cent own 47 per cent of such wealth and the top 20 per cent hold 91 per cent. In Britain the Commission on Taxation and Citizenship (2000) records wealth is more unequally distributed than income and that the trend of wealth inequality has been worsening over recent times. It notes that the proportion of total marketable wealth held by the wealthiest 10 per cent of the population rose from 49 per cent in 1982 to around 52 per cent in 1999. The material covered in this chapter is valuable even if one is interested more narrowly on wealth taxes rather different ways of funding the assets agenda.

The structure of this chapter is as follows. The next section sets out details of the focus group methods used in this study. After this the chapter presents results from the focus group discussions, looking first at views towards wealth taxes and then at attitudes towards different ways of funding an inclusive assets policy. A discussion then draws together some of the main themes to emerge from the focus groups.

Focus groups

Focus group methods were used in this study. The selection of the focus groups was shaped by previous empirical and theoretical research. Survey evidence suggests that younger people are more hostile to inheritance tax than older people (Commission on

Taxation and Citizenship 2000; Hedges and Bromley 2001). It is perhaps unsurprising that those who are most likely to receive an inheritance, namely the young, are also more opposed to attempts to tax inheritances. Empirical research also suggests that people on lower incomes are more opposed to inheritance taxes than those on higher incomes (Commission on Taxation and Citizenship 2000; Lewis and White 2006). This could occur for a variety of reasons. For example, those who currently have little may be more sensitive to efforts by government to take resources away from individuals, even if this means giving to others. To take account of the differences between age and income, focus groups were convened along the lines of age and income. A professional market research company was used to recruit these groups. These groups were spread over the north and south of England. Age was divided into a younger (18–39 years old) and older (40+) band. These bands were chosen to correspond to the bands used in previous investigations of inheritance tax (Hedges and Bromley 2001). The younger age groups were all pre-children and the older groups did not have children who received the Child Trust Fund. This allowed these groups to be clearly distinguished from the Child Trust Fund groups (detailed below). The cut-off point for personal income was set at roughly the level of household income used to separate recipients of a £500 and £250 Child Trust Fund. This was chosen to limit the variability across groups. Personal rather than household income was chosen to accommodate lone parent households that have a personal income close to the cut-off point for the higher endowment.

Focus groups were also convened with parents who receive the Child Trust Fund vouchers. In Britain, the Child Trust Fund serves as the centre of policy debates about how to deliver an expanded citizen's stake (Paxton, White and Maxwell 2006). Consequently, it was appropriate to examine the Child Trust Fund when exploring the assets approach. Talking with parents was useful as it provided the perspective of one of the key users of the Child Trust Fund to various proposals from the policy world to boost the Child Trust Fund. Focus groups with parents were also valuable for theoretical reasons. Asset-based social theory predicts that asset-ownership changes the way that people think about the world (Sherraden 1991; Paxton 2003). It might be that the provision of a Child Trust Fund would have led parents to think differently about wealth inequality. Two focus groups were convened with parents who receive the Child Trust Fund. These groups were based at Sure Start centres, one in the north and the other in the south of England. To help isolate any asset effect, a focus group was also conducted with parents of young children who do not receive the Child Trust Fund to examine their views about addressing wealth inequality (this is designated as a 'no Child Trust Fund' group).

There were seven groups in this study, covering 58 participants. These groups were convened in the summer of 2006. Both men and women participated in this study. There were more women than men because the two focus groups convened with parents who receive the Child Trust Fund contained more women than men. All other groups had roughly equal numbers of men and women. All participants were paid, and discussions usually lasted about an hour.

A common set of questions was asked in all of the groups. These questions focused on two main themes. First, people's attitudes towards wealth taxes. Part of this examined views about inheritance tax. Perhaps the most popular type of wealth tax endorsed within the British policy community is some form of inheritance tax (Atkinson 1972; Commission on Taxation and Citizenship 2000; Maxwell 2004). The groups were initially asked about their views about inheritance tax. This was to establish a baseline against which the subsequent discussion could be judged.

Chapter 1 indicated that inheritance tax appears to be particularly unpopular among the general population. This chapter considers various suggestions that have been made about how to counter this unpopularity. Some commentators suggest that 'stories' rather than 'science' could enhance public support for wealth taxes (Graetz and Shapiro 2005; Commission on Life Chances and Child Poverty 2006). For example, Michael Graetz and Ian Shapiro (2005) argue that in the United States a large part of the success that conservatives enjoyed in gaining mass support for repealing an estates tax is due to the way that they used evocative case histories of hard-working families hit by inheritance taxes to advance their cause. Graetz and Shapiro continue that while progressives tried to counter attack on wealth taxes by marshalling statistics and facts, conservatives had greater success by appealing to well-spun stories (whatever the accuracy of such stories in reality). These authors suggest that if progressives act in a similar fashion then public attitudes might be quite different. They say that the, 'opponents of reform never tried to shift the rhetoric away from the hard-working business owners and farmers to those who benefit most from inherited wealth – the rich children who are born on third base yet behave as though they have hit triples' (Graetz and Shapiro 2005, 233).

The groups were then used to explore Graetz's and Shapiro's suggestion of using Paris Hilton as a focus for a story, as well as a different story proposed by the Commission on Life Chances and Child Poverty (2006) that centres on 'life chances'. The Commission reports that deliberative work it commissioned discovered two types of story that undermine public support for progressive policies. 'Origin stories' focus on people from humble backgrounds who manage to acquire riches. Such stories were thought to indicate that poverty does not limit material progress. The second type of story concentrates on the 'feckless poor'. This blames the poor for their predicament, for example, by suggesting that they are lazy and work-shy. The Commission argues that a revolution in empathy is needed towards poverty. The Commission suggests that a narrative that centres on the struggles that hard-working families in providing equal life chances for their children could provide one such story.

The discussion of inheritance tax also examined people's attitudes when offered a choice between cuts in income tax or estates tax. A.B. Atkinson (1972) argues that it is important when discussing tax policy to look how a particular tax fits alongside other taxes. With this in mind, the focus groups were presented with the following choice: a lower income tax but a higher estates tax or a higher income tax but a lower estates tax. Income tax was chosen to inform this choice because empirical research suggests that the view that a tax on transfers of wealth constitutes a 'double tax' over the income tax a person pays is a major source of dissatisfaction with estates tax (Lewis and White 2006).

The examination of wealth taxes also studied an alternative to inheritance or estates tax that has recently gathered interest, namely a land tax (Maxwell and Vigor 2005; Wilcox 2005; McLean 2006). Iain McLean (2006) argues that the apparent hostility to inheritance tax means it is worthwhile to look at how other taxes might be used to fund an expanded citizen's stake. He suggests that a different wealth tax based on land value taxation could be used instead as way of paying for an increased Child Trust Fund.

The second theme of the focus groups explored public attitudes towards alternatives to wealth taxes. Part of this looked at a community fund idea whereby the government establishes a national pot of money that is then invested by an independent set of financial advisors on the stock market (Holtham 1999). The returns to the investment are used to replenish the fund for future years as well as pay for spending programmes, which in this case is a more generous Child Trust Fund. The remainder of the questions looked at views about using cuts in public expenditure elsewhere rather than additional taxation as a way of paying for an enhanced stake. Michael Sherraden (1991) argues that when discussing this it is better to focus on potential spending cuts from welfare programmes rather than other areas as this is likely to be a more realistic way of paying for assets. Howard Glennerster and Abigail McKnight (2006) argue that one of the few areas that spending cuts could be justified is in higher education. University funding is generally regressive as it consists of a subsidy to students who were often already from comfortable backgrounds and that once a student leaves university they benefit directly from their education through higher wages over their counterparts who have not gone to university. Participants were asked if they supported cutting government spending on universities as a way of paying for an expanded stake. The focus groups were also used to explore examples of spending cuts from areas of health and pension provision that have provoked recent controversy, looking specifically at proposals to reduce general practitioner pay or raise the public sector pension age to remove any disparity in the retirement ages between the public and private sectors to generate funds for a larger stake.

Results

Government inefficiency

The discussion of wealth taxes and alternatives to wealth taxes was conducted against general resistance to paying more taxes or supporting spending cuts. A common view was that ample funds could be made available simply by cutting out government inefficiency. Government and civil servants were thought to be wasteful, and removing this waste would mean that funds could be raised without the need for further taxes or spending cuts. For some respondents, this was their preferred way of paying for assets. They challenged the options that they were presented with (namely, inheritance tax, land tax, community fund or spending cuts) and stated their favoured option was to drive out inefficiency. People did not usually identify specific areas of inefficiency but rather pointed to general government wastefulness.

- *Male, low income, West Yorkshire*
  [The] whole discussion is based on an assumption that I can't accept, that we need to raise more money and I think you're getting more than enough out of us. I just can't accept the fact that you try and find ways, the government is trying to find ways of increasing the amount of tax that we're having to pay. I think that we're paying enough. We're paying more than enough and we ain't getting value for money.

Although these sentiments were acknowledged, the focus groups were asked that if people had to raise more money from taxes or spending cuts then which of the presented options they would favour. The aim was to go beyond broad perceptions of waste and concentrate on attitudes to specific policies, such as inheritance tax or land tax. The responses below should be set against, however, general resistance to extra tax or spending cuts.

Wealth taxes

Inheritance tax

In common with previous studies, there was marked hostility towards inheritance tax. This opposition was exhibited across all of the groups. 'Double taxation' was cited as one of the main reasons for unhappiness with inheritance tax. People felt that they had paid income tax throughout their life and so any tax on their estate was an unfair double tax.

- *Male, no Child Trust Fund, Surrey*
  You pay tax all through your working life and then hopefully for your children, hopefully if you've done well or been successful you want to leave something for your children or your grandchildren if you've got them and then some bugger comes and takes it. You've worked all of your life for it, it's wrong. Totally wrong.

People also expressed concern that rising house prices meant that ordinary hard-working families would now be liable to pay inheritance tax. Most felt that the threshold at which inheritance tax starts ought to be raised, to at least £500,000 which was seen as double the average house price. People also felt that the 40 per cent rate was high and should not be raised any further. Moreover, arguments were heard for reducing the rate, particularly when someone first passes the inheritance tax threshold.

Double taxation refers to the idea that inheritance tax is an extra (second) tax over income tax. This feature of double taxation is not unique to inheritance tax but refers to any sort of tax additional to income tax. Thus, VAT or duties on petrol could also be considered double taxation. To see whether the double taxation objection was directed at multiple taxation or whether it was a convenient way to criticise inheritance tax, people were asked whether they also objected to paying VAT on grounds of double taxation. Opinion was split over this question. Some complained about VAT in the same manner. The tax system was described as complicated and there was a desire for the tax system to be made simpler by streamlining taxes. It was put to the group that if people objected to double taxation then this implies that there should only be one tax. This attracted the support of a minority of the participants. Others were not opposed to VAT on double taxation grounds and attempted to provide justifications for VAT. One view was that VAT implied an element of choice that was missing with inheritance tax, and this meant a case for VAT that was missing in inheritance tax.

- *Male, 18–39, higher income, West Yorkshire*
  Purchasing the product which you pay VAT on is an active thing that you choose to do ...if you're buying DVD players, large things, whatever, you are choosing to do that.

Attitudes to inheritance tax were therefore complex. Although there was substantial opposition to inheritance tax on grounds of double taxation, there was evidence that this was part of a wider concern with all sorts of taxes. That said, inheritance tax did seem to arouse particular opposition, and in part this was because there was a strong commitment to the view that parents should be allowed to pass on their wealth to their children.

Paris Hilton benefit fund

The discussion of wealth taxes and assets was conducted against the background of broad antipathy towards inheritance tax. The view that parents should be allowed to pass on the fruits of their labour to their children was often invoked in discussions of inheritance tax. To see whether the relationship between parents and children could be viewed in a different way, two stories were suggested to the groups. The first story used recommendations made by Michael Graetz and Ian Shapiro (2005) to shift attention to the recipient of an inheritance, and use a story based on someone due to inherit a fortune. They suggest that Paris Hilton could be used to construct such a story. People were asked if they thought it fair that people like Paris Hilton did not have to work while most families have to work for their living. It was also noted that in the United States cutting estates tax is said to amount effectively to a 'Paris Hilton Benefit Act', and why should government give tax-breaks to the super-rich.

Although the Paris Hilton story did have some impact, most participants were still opposed to inheritance tax. The belief that parents should be allowed to transfer the wealth to their children was not easy to budge. Two views were offered in favour of Paris Hilton. First, her parents had already paid tax on the money and so it was unfair to impose another tax on the money. People were unmoved by the counter that while her parents might have worked hard, she hadn't.

- *Female, Child Trust Fund, London*
  But her mum and dad worked hard for that money, you know what I mean, someone has worked hard for that money, they're leaving it to their daughter, son, family. So if they've worked hard for it, why should it be taxed? It's been taxed already.
- *Male, 18–39, lower income, Surrey*
  I mean at the end of the day somewhere along the line someone has worked really hard for that, I mean whatever the weather, you either get lucky or you don't.

Second, participants challenged the view that Paris Hilton would not be taxed. The view here was that she is liable to pay various taxes as soon as she starts spending her inheritance or puts it into savings or investments. The prospect of such taxes was used as a counterweight to imposing an inheritance tax on Paris Hilton.

- *Female, Child Trust Fund, West Yorkshire*
  But you will later. So if you put it in any savings, you're going to get tax on it. So you will get taxed on it as you go through your life. It won't be the lump-sum that you got that's tax-free. If you put it in your savings, or if you invest with it, you're going to get taxed on it to a degree.

Life chances

The second story drew on the suggestion made by the Commission on Life Chances and Child Poverty that looked at the struggles of ordinary hard-working families in supporting their children. The life-chances approach attracted more sympathetic views in the focus groups, particularly among parents who receive the Child Trust Fund as well as the group of parents with young children with no Child Trust Fund. This story was associated with a more positive message than the previous story. However, this did not mean that there was a sea change in attitudes to inheritance tax. Opposition to inheritance tax though lessened was not overturned.

- *Female, Child Trust Fund, West Yorkshire*
  I can see the logic behind it because if you're taking it as a society there's some people who are more able to generate wealth and so you're going to end up with an uneven situation with mega-rich people and the rest who aren't. The idea of trying to even things out when people die, that does make sense. I mean that does make sense. But on the other hand, the reason why there seems to be something unpleasant about it is because that money's within families and there's something about money and families being ours, you know, we worked for this and why should it be taken away from our family. To a large extent people work for their children or grandchildren.

More critical individuals questioned whether this approach would work in practice as this would drive wealth creators out of the country. In several groups the life-chances approach was criticised as verging on communism.

- *Female, no Child Trust Fund, Surrey*
  It sounds ideal, it sounds a lovely, nicely, nicely idea ...[but]... I tend to agree that people are greedy and it wouldn't work, you know, people would move out of the country.
- *Male, 18–39, higher income, West Yorkshire*
  Its almost like communism isn't it ... everybody is not equal, there are some people who work a lot harder than other people and it's unfair to penalise someone just because they've done really well.

Although evidence in the groups suggested that stories could help increase support for inheritance tax, this was not sufficient to overturn initial opposition to inheritance tax.

Income tax versus inheritance tax

To explore attitudes to inheritance tax further, participants were asked to comment on whether they preferred a higher income tax over their lifetime but a lower tax on their final estate, or a lower income tax over their life but a higher inheritance tax. This question was aimed at seeing whether attitudes to inheritance taxes would change when these taxes were considered alongside other taxes. The discussion of double taxation indicated the existence of broader concerns with the tax system, and the purpose here was to build on these sentiments. This question was associated with the largest shift of opinion over inheritance tax. Opinion was divided in the groups over these options. Some individuals favoured paying a higher income tax during their lifetime and their descendants incurring a lower inheritance tax over the alternative of a lower income tax but a higher inheritance tax.

- *Male, 40+, higher income, Surrey*
  A higher income tax because really what these people are doing metaphorically speaking is burying their treasure and then they want to give it up and give the whole thing for their kids. But this is their treasure and they don't want anyone to interfere with that.

However, a significant strand of opinion opted to reduce their income tax and allow the descendants to pay a higher inheritance tax. Although this view was not in the majority in any of the groups, it nevertheless marked a departure from the near unanimous opposition to inheritance tax expressed at the beginning of the groups. One argument was that the money people earned themselves was theirs, and so they had the right to enjoy it.

> • *Male, 40+, lower income, West Yorkshire*
> *Why are people always obsessed with always leaving things for your children? Everybody likes leaving things for your children, I would do the same, but it becomes your obsession, you must do it. You spend your money, you enjoy it.*

Some individuals stated while they supported a lower income tax they nevertheless felt some qualms because they felt they were acting selfishly. In the groups of young people without children, some individuals reported that if they had children in the future they might think differently about opting for a lower income tax.

> • *Female, 18–39, higher income, West Yorkshire*
> *At the time of my life that I'm at now I do, but I'm sure in twenty years when I'm married with children then I might feel differently. But at the moment I've only got to think about myself, I know that sounds really selfish, but my salary at the end of my month is mine. I've got my own house on my own, I live my life, and really, really selfishly, if it's going to give me more money in my monthly salary I'll take it. I know it sounds selfish, but in twenty-five years if I've got kids, then of course I want to leave them something.*

The groups of parents with young children, however, exhibited a similar pattern of opinion to other groups and were not more likely to opt for paying a higher income tax and lower inheritance tax. Indeed, arguments were voiced within these groups about the way that lower income tax might in fact help parents bring up young children by freeing up more money to give to their children while they are living.

> • *Female, no Child Trust Fund, Surrey*
> *I'd have the lower income tax ...because otherwise you're going to be struggling all your life, with your children, so it's not just like you struggling. If you're struggling, they're struggling. If you can't provide*

for them then you will suffer. You're better to do that and then hopefully they'll get jobs and ok they'll get stung when you pop your clogs and they won't get as much but at least they'll have lived comfortably until they're old enough to stand on their own two feet.

Land tax

The discussion of wealth taxes then considered an alternative to wealth taxes in the guise of a land tax. Drawing on Ian McLean (2006), participants were asked to consider a situation in which their local council gives planning permission for some new investment near their home (such as a brand new supermarket or new public transport link), and this enhances the value of their property by a substantial amount (say £100,000). It was explained that a tax placed on the value of their property would mean they would be liable for more tax, although they would also capture some of the increase in the value of their property as a result of investment for which they were not directly responsible. Generally speaking, people reacted more favourably to a land tax than inheritance tax. A land tax avoided the misgivings people had with inheritance tax about the state taxing wealth that parents wished to pass on to their children. There was a recognition of the fairness of a land tax.

- *Male, 18–39, lower income, Surrey*
  I think it's pretty fair. The fact that it's something that's out of your hands, but it's improved your areas, but you're going to get a profit, it doesn't matter that they're going to take some out of it. It seems irrelevant, the fact that you're going to get profit, something you didn't do but it's increased the value of your property.

This is not to say that a land tax attracted no criticism. The fairness of a land tax was challenged in most groups, with people claiming that any profits on their home are rightfully theirs whether or not they were responsible for the investment. People also stated that while councils were happy to take more tax from a home-owner if the property price rises, they are sceptical that councils would reduce the tax bill if they built something next door that depresses the value of their home. A different concern was over the affordability of land tax. In particular, people were worried that their income may not be sufficient to pay for the land tax increases, particularly where property price increases outstripped increases in their income.

- *Male, 18–39, higher income, West Yorkshire*
  I think the general concept is fine, but I think the only problem that you have is lets say you've got a house that happens to be situated ...[in an] ...up and coming area, so in five years say the area has turned really into somewhere really nice, the house price has doubled. You've no desire to move, you don't want to move, your income has not changed necessarily that much, yet at this point because your areas has succeeded, you are now paying double the thing you were paying before, just as an arbitrary figure. Whilst I appreciate as a general concept that paying more because your property is worth more seems perfectly fair, there are situations like that when you are being penalised for suddenly the fact that the area's changed around you.

Alternatives to wealth taxes

Community fund

The community fund idea was the most popular of the presented options (inheritance tax, land tax, community fund, and spending cuts) for raising additional funds. People liked the idea that this pot of money would be dedicated for the benefit of the nation, and individuals in several groups likened the community element to the National Lottery. Individuals did not seem to regard the fund as taking anything away from them and contrasted this with wealth taxes or cuts in public spending.

- *Female, 18–39, higher income, West Yorkshire*
  That's a fantastic idea as long as they're earning money from it.

Although the response was broadly positive, respondents raised several issues about this policy. First, although people accepted the investment of collective funds on the stock-market, concerns were expressed about the possibility of stock-market crashes and the impact this could have on the fund.

Second, people questioned whether government would have the competence to spend the proceeds of the fund wisely and indeed whether government could be trusted to use money for the stated purposes.

- *Male, 40+, lower income, West Yorkshire*
  I think it sounds like a good idea as long as it's spent wisely, but we end up with another [Millennium] dome thing?

Third, some individuals queried whether the money from the fund should be used to boost the Child Trust Fund. Although individuals generally agreed that boosting the Child Trust Fund was a reasonable way of spending the money, some felt that money would be better spent on the National Health Service.

- *Female, no Child Trust Fund, Surrey*
  There's more important things I think like people who are sick and can't get treatment on the NHS ...I know Child Trust Fund is a lovely idea, but I just think there's more important things that need to be addressed with that money.

Individuals were then asked to comment on an idea of raising the initial money for the community fund. It was explained that the community fund would require start-up funds, and it was suggested this could come from a one-off tax that is placed on the shares of companies. Most people backed this, saying that those in the position to pay for shares can afford to contribute to the initial money into the fund.

- *Male, 18–39, lower income, Surrey*
  If you're buying shares, you're obviously at that higher class level financially and it's not taking off the people that are really working their socks off to provide for their family, their inheritance.

Cuts in public spending

Higher education

The discussion of spending cuts as an alternative to additional taxes or the community fund was shaped by a general reluctance to countenance spending cuts. People usually provided reasons why a particular area should not be cut rather than why a specific area should be used to generate savings. There was broad hostility to the idea of cutting the public subsidy to higher education as this was thought to undermine the future of the nation. Information about the regressive nature of university funding did not appear to alter people's views.

- *Male, 40+, higher income, Surrey*
  What you've got is a situation where you've got very bright children, very bright kids who are the country's future and you want to cut their educational allowance so that kids then don't have the incentive to learn. So the brightness of the country, the bright future of the country is diminished. What's the investment in that? The long term investment, we should be encouraging people to learn and go to university, not cutting everything from under their feet.

The two groups of lower income individuals (18–39, 40+) were more receptive than the other groups towards cutting university funds. This was more the case for the younger group, and for those who had not been to university.

- *Male, 18–39, lower income, Surrey*
  I agree with that, I think universities are a waste of time. They're going there, they're going there for random degrees and they are coming out and no one will employ them because they have got no experience. I know someone that went to university, they got honours, but now they're an electrician because nobody will take him in.

Although lower income groups were more likely to support such cuts, these views were still not in the majority in these groups.

GP pay

In Britain, general practitioners have recently been awarded with generous pay settlements (in 2006 the average wage was reported to be £106,000 a year).[1] The idea was to see whether people believe that some public servants were paid too much and it would be better if these individuals received less and the savings generated could be used for a wider public benefit.

People were asked if they were willing to support cuts in GP pay to generate funds. Generally individuals were against this idea, arguing that GPs had worked hard for their money and so government was not entitled to cut this.

- *Female, Child Trust Fund, London*
  They're so overworked anyway, I think they deserve that money. They go to school to learn medicine, to help save someone's life, hundreds of patients to see every week, and they deserve that money because they've worked hard for it.

Pension age

A third option looked at a disparity in pension ages between those in the public and private sectors. Some public servants can retire earlier than those in the private sector. The idea was to see if this difference between the public and private sectors was a source of tension and unpopularity, and so closing the gap by raising the public sector age could be used to make cost savings that could be used to generate funds.

Views were more mixed about the prospect of raising the public sector pension age as a way of saving money. Some individuals argued that part of the deal of working in the public sector is that public servants accepted a lower wage than they would get in the private sector in return for the promise that they could retire at an earlier age. Others challenged this, saying that recently public sector workers have enjoyed generous wage increases and that fairness dictates that the people should have the same retirement age within the public and private sectors.

- *Male, Child Trust Fund, West Yorkshire*
  Why should say if it's me and you, we're both the same age, why should I have to work 5 years more than you to get the same amount of benefits. You're going to get the same amount of benefits as what I'm going to get in 5 years time, so it should be level all the way round.

There was no strong desire, however, about closing the gap in retirement ages as a way of raising money.

Discussion and conclusions

This chapter has presented original evidence on paying for assets. The results are from a small-scale qualitative study and so care should be taken not to exaggerate the impact of these findings. Nevertheless, some tentative conclusions can be drawn from these discussions.

First, criticisms of wealth taxes were part of a broader concern with all taxes. A common notion among the groups was that taxes are currently not being spent well. People were generally wary of all taxes, not just wealth taxes. Government is often thought to be wasteful and profligate. This means that the challenge of persuading people to support wealth taxes is not of a completely different order as that posed by other taxes. Although wealth taxes do not present a different category of problem, there was nevertheless evidence in the focus groups that people exhibited greater resistance to inheritance tax than other taxes. For example, the discussion of double taxation indicated that people tended to be more opposed to inheritance tax than VAT. The idea that parents should be allowed to pass on wealth to their children exerted an important hold on the imagination, and inheritance tax was thought to undermine this in ways that taxes such as VAT do not.

Second, the way that wealth taxes are 'framed' appears to affect support for these taxes. Wealth taxes are subject to different arguments. The life-chances approach provides one argument for ensuring a greater equality of inheritances. A different argument highlights the importance of allowing parents to bequeath wealth to their children to cement the family unit. Faced with competing arguments, individuals often responded to those arguments that could be presented in an evocative manner. As noted above, the view that parents should be allowed to pass wealth onto their offspring was an idea with powerful appeal. This did not mean that the attitudes of people could not be budged. Opposition to inheritance tax weakened when people were presented with an alternative story about providing families with equal chances for their children. However, even more important was when individuals were offered a choice between income tax and inheritance tax. This illustrated that while participants responded to narratives based around the family, these could be shaped in a number of ways. The choice of income tax versus inheritance tax complicated the link people made between parents and children. It opened up debates about the interests of parents versus those of children, as well as different ways that parents could help children other than transferring wealth at death.

Some argued that a lower income tax would allow parents to give more money to the children when they are living. Although stories about the family were important, they did not have to be conducted solely through the idea of parents bequeathing wealth to future generations.

Third, some types of wealth tax provoked greater support than others. In particular, land tax appeared to be less contentious than inheritance tax. The main reason for this seemed to be that land tax avoided controversies surrounding the family that was associated with inheritance tax. Many of the complaints about the land tax were about practical aspects of this policy, namely whether councils could be trusted to reduce the tax bill in event of house price falls and what would happen if rises in personal income did not keep up with house price inflation.

Fourth, the community fund idea was the most popular of the presented options provided for raising money. Stuart White (2006) presents a community fund as part of a long-term strategy for assets and states that this initiative is likely to be 'wildly utopian' by contemporary standards. However, participants in the focus groups responded more positively to this idea than wealth taxes or spending cuts. Part of this seemed to be driven by the perception that this was the least costly option to themselves, in that it did not require additional taxes or for individuals to suffer cuts in public services. People were also more inclined to associate the community fund with a positive message, that is creating something for the good of the national community. The support for the community fund did not translate automatically into support for assets. Although the Child Trust Fund was deemed an acceptable way of spending money from the community fund, there were arguments that proceeds from the community fund would be better spent on the NHS. The support for assets, thus, was not very deep. Nonetheless, on balance an inclusive assets policy based around a community fund seems a better bet than wealth taxes as a way of tackling wealth inequality. At the end of the focus groups when people were asked to choose among inheritance tax, land tax, community fund or spending cuts as a way of funding assets, the most common response was for a community fund.

Fifth, people seemed just as resistant to cuts in public services as they were to additional taxes. People were wary of losing any public services even if this meant funding increases elsewhere. Any problems experienced with public services were ascribed to government mismanagement, and generally people felt that tackling waste could generate funds without having to cut services. Reallocating expenditure seems just as difficult as rolling back the frontiers of the state.

A policy based on a community fund seemed to be the preferred choice from the menu of options offered within this focus group study. This does not mean that there is no potential in other policies. There appears to be scope for extending wealth taxes, particularly if they are framed appropriately. Drawing on this idea, one way of progressing with a community fund idea is to develop narratives or evocative stories of how the community fund could be used to create a society based on equal life chances.

7
Conclusion

Introduction

This book has examined the assets agenda. This is an area of policy that emphasises the stock of assets owned by individuals. Asset-based initiatives have caught the imagination of politicians and policy-makers across the world. In the introductory chapter I identified two key problems, however, that exist with this agenda. First, there is considerable confusion at a theoretical level. The assets agenda is composed of different parts but there is often a failure to distinguish between these different elements. This confusion is an obstacle to progress as it means that individuals are often talking at cross-purposes. Second, the stock of empirical knowledge is small. Although data on asset policies is growing, it remains fairly small. This means that efforts to roll out assets at a policy level often lack a solid empirical foundation.

This book has sought to address both of these issues. Chapters 2 to 4 concentrated on the first deficiency, by studying the assets agenda within the realms of social policy and citizenship. This discussion indicated the complexity and variety of asset policies, both in different types of social policy approach and different models of citizenship. One implication of this is that care should be taken about which particular agenda one is referring to when examining the assets agenda. Arguments about social policy differ from those of citizenship. The quality of debates would be improved if one does not slide between different theoretical branches of the assets agenda. The diversity of the assets approach also means that one can discard one part of the assets agenda without rejecting this wholesale. For example, it is possible to reject social policy approaches while also believing that the ownership of assets is a worthwhile aspect of citizenship (or vice versa).

Asset-based ideas open up interesting debates, either by charting new lines of enquiry or by reviving older arguments that have been neglected. The social policy wing can be seen as part of a broader contemporary effort to 're-state' the state. The state has often been conceived in a centralised fashion. This means that the state is understood to be the monopoly funder and provider of welfare services. Of course the reality of the welfare state has often differed radically from this conception, with a considerable role for private or non-state agencies in the funding and delivery of public services. This complex picture should not detract, however, from the fact that the centralised state has nevertheless had an important hold on the imagination in the policy community (Prabhakar 2006). Today this state-centred model is being re-examined. This is driven by intellectual challenges from neoliberals and other parts of the 'New Right' as well as changing social and economic conditions such as globalisation. Asset-based welfare forms part of this rethinking, and its emphasis on productive investments implies a change in the role of the state from being a direct provider to an investor or enabler.

Models of citizenship also create space for interesting debates about the new politics of ownership. This revives a stream of radical political thought from the 18th century and specifically the arguments of figures such as Thomas Paine. Gareth Stedman Jones (2004) argues that Paine's arguments promised a new political economy that transcended the divisions between left and right. Stedman Jones states that Paine's ideas were ultimately stifled by the political fallout from the French revolution. This revolution polarised opinion between left and right, and this squeezed out Paine's ideas (Stedman Jones 2004). The models advanced by Bruce Ackerman, Anne Alstott and Stuart White renew this line of thought. Whether this will add up to a new political economy remains to be seen. However, the new politics of ownership at least creates a space for interesting debates. The assets agenda specifically opens up discussions about how property is spread throughout society and economy. Instead of allowing a society in which there are large concentrations of property in a few hands and no property belonging to the many, the assets agenda insists that ownership should be distributed more widely. This model of private property has the potential to cut across political divisions and create a programme with mass appeal. Chapters 5 and 6 addressed the second defect of the assets agenda. These chapters add to the current stock of empirical knowledge by providing data on a concrete example of a universal assets policy as well as information on how assets could be paid for in the future. Chapter 4 presented evidence on parental attitudes to the Child Trust Fund. Several broad themes can be identified from these discussions. First, assets form a policy approach with potential mass appeal. Identifying policies that have a genuinely wide appeal is not an easy task. Often, sizeable constituencies can be detected within the public for or against a particular policy. The focus group on the Child Trust Fund suggests that asset policies could be one area that will attract broad swathes of the population. Most respondents liked the Child Trust Fund. Worries were expressed about the particular way that the Child Trust Fund has been crafted. However, this needs to be set against general support for this policy.

Second, difficulties are likely to be encountered when moving from theory to practice. The Child Trust Fund is a fairly simple policy: this provides a capital endowment to all children. Nevertheless, this policy still aroused concern. Disquiet was voiced about the information surrounding this policy as well as the treatment of older siblings. There are no straightforward answers to these issues. However, the more complex an assets policy is, the greater the difficulties that are likely to be encountered when moving from theory to practice.

Third, the public did not have an appetite for using assets to replace other forms of welfare intervention. People liked assets, but not at the expense of cutting income benefits or public services. There was support for a mix policy stance that included income, assets and public services. This should define the future development of asset policies.

Chapter 6 looked at different ways of paying for an enhanced citizen's stake. Two general points can be made about these discussions. First, raising extra money for asset policies, or indeed any other sort of policy, is not an easy matter. Of course, this might be peculiar to Britain, as the public in countries elsewhere might be more receptive to higher taxes. However, the evidence presented here suggests that there is a perception that taxes are not being spent well and people were resistant to paying more taxes or endorsing cuts in public services.

Second, there is potential for reform. The public resistance should not be a counsel of despair. There is scope for increasing support for wealth taxes, particularly if evocative stories back up the extra tax claims. Proving people with concrete choices may help reveal underlying preferences about specific taxes. More strikingly, there was interest in a community fund idea. This idea has interested parts of the policy community and people responded positively to this proposal. A community fund is an example of a form of collective ownership being used to back individual ownership. This underlines that one of the most potent aspects of the assets agenda is the impulse it provides to new debates about ownership.

A liberal welfare policy?

Looking now to the future, what are the prospects for the assets agenda being extended as part of public policy? One noticeable feature of the assets agenda is that it is currently most closely associated with the 'Anglo-Saxon' or 'liberal welfare' world encompassing the United States, Canada, Australia, Britain and New Zealand. If there is a necessary connection between assets and liberal welfare regimes, then this would stop the assets agenda being adopted more generally.

Gosta Esping-Andersen's (2002; 2004) work outlines the different worlds of welfare capitalism. Esping-Andersen argues that there are three main types of welfare system, namely liberal, conservative or social democratic systems. These worlds differ according to the nature and extent of social rights; the stance towards equality; and the emphasis placed on the state, market or family within the welfare system. He says that while most countries combine elements of these different types, different countries are nevertheless biased towards different types. Esping-Andersen states that liberal regimes predominate in the United States, Britain, Australia and Canada. Means-tested benefits feature prominently in the provision of rights, and there is concern with eradicating poverty rather than inequality. Liberal regimes tend to favour use of markets over the state or families within the welfare system. Esping-Andersen argues that conservative systems tend to occur in places such as Germany or southern Europe. There is a broader notion of social rights than in liberal regimes, although this system is geared towards maintaining hierarchies within society. The family is seen as a key foundation for welfare policy. Finally, Esping-Andersen highlights social democratic systems. He states that these are associated most closely with countries such as Sweden and Denmark. These systems favour the provision of a generous set of universal rights and are committed to promoting a broad notion of equality. The state is a major player within social democratic regimes.

There is currently a close association between assets and those countries with strong liberal welfare traditions. Much of the intellectual case for assets occurs in the United States and Britain, in the writings of Bruce Ackerman, Anne Alstott, Stuart White, Michael Sherraden, Julian Le Grand, Samuel Bowles and Herbert Gintis. The most developed policies, such as the Child Trust Fund and Individual Development Accounts, arise in the Anglo-Saxon world. Finally, the greatest political interest is exhibited by politicians such as George Bush in the United States, David Blunkett in Britain and Helen Clark in New Zealand. One viewpoint is that this association is not accidental: individualism is key to liberal welfare policy and assets fit this because they are oriented towards the individual. Commenting on a proposal to provide special accounts for those who care for others, Jane Lewis states that, 'Care accounts represent a highly individualised solution most suited to systems that are already heavily reliant on the private sector and the private sphere of the family. There is therefore good reason why much of the debate on this issue is American' (Lewis 2006, 164).

An obvious qualification to the above view is that asset-based ideas do not emerge only in the Anglo-Saxon world. Chapter 1 noted interest in personal welfare accounts in social democratic Sweden and I shall consider below proposals for 'sabbatical accounts' that allow people to take a break or sabbatical from their normal working lives in conservative Germany. Furthermore, the Centre for Social Development in St Louis and the Washington D.C. based think-tank the New America Foundation has embarked on a global assets project that seeks to extend asset policies in Africa, Asia and South America, covering countries such as Uganda, Taiwan,

Hong Kong, Indonesia, Columbia and Peru (Chowa 2007; Cheng 2007; Sherraden and Zou 2007; Sherraden and Zou 2006; Moury 2006). For example, in Indonesia the Center for Social Development worked alongside the Ministry of Social Welfare and academics from the State Islamic University to design a 5-year pilot project due to run from 2006 to 2010. The initiative is based on Individual Development Accounts and focuses on 'DAPIs' (which in Bahasa Indonesian stands for Dana Abadi Pengembangan Individu, which translates as 'funds for everlasting individual development'). The pilot is based in four provinces and is aimed at supporting 665 accounts dedicated for enterprise, 660 accounts for education and 660 accounts for housing (Sherraden and Zou 2006). Individual Development Accounts also inform two pilots projects in Peru. A 6-year project running from 2005 to 2011 is aimed at increasing savings among poor women in southern Peru. Savings made by more than 5,000 women attract matching grants. To qualify for the scheme, women have to open a personal saving account, increase their monthly savings and use the asset to pay for education, health, housing or starting a business. A Southern Highlands project that started in 2005 aims to extend this by creating accounts for 37,000 women (Moury 2006).

Of course, these instances do not in themselves defeat the view that the assets agenda is an Anglo-Saxon phenomenon or an attempt to export liberal policies to other countries. These apparent counterexamples might simply reflect the hybrid nature of most welfare states. Gosta Esping-Andersen acknowledges that his different worlds of welfare capitalism are 'ideal types'. That is, these types represent the different bundles of ideas and policies that can be distinguished at an analytical or intellectual level. In reality, most countries contain elements from each of the different worlds of welfare capitalism, and consequently are hybrid welfare regimes. The presence of asset initiatives in Sweden and Germany might comprise the liberal features of their own welfare systems.

The analysis in this book opposes the view that the asset agenda is the exclusive preserve of the Anglo-Saxon world. Although there is presently a close connection between assets and the liberal welfare policy, this agenda is compatible with other welfare traditions. This can be seen more clearly if one separates out different wings of the assets agenda. Gosta Esping-Andersen associates liberal models with targeted benefits, a lack of concern with equality and an emphasis on the market. It is possible to develop some versions of asset-based social policy that share these characteristics. Such policies might be targeted at particular sections of the population; aimed at reducing absolute poverty rather than inequality; and acquired and deployed voluntarily through the market. However, other versions of asset-based welfare might have none of these elements and have more in common with social democratic rather than liberal worlds. A social democratic model could emphasise universal schemes, contain progressive elements (such as matched savings elements for low income individuals), and the state could have a substantial role in redistributing property to guarantee assets for all. The view that asset-based welfare should only be seen as an example of liberal welfare can therefore be contested. The break with liberal welfare is clearer with the citizenship wing of the assets agenda. Citizenship models are universal and not means-tested; have a commitment to equality as a foundation for freedom; and have a significant role for the state in securing assets for all. Citizenship rather than social policy is potentially more attractive beyond the Anglo-Saxon world, and is a dimension along which asset policies could be extended.

Sabbatical accounts

The potential of the assets agenda being extended beyond the Anglo-Saxon world can be seen in the interest shown to sabbatical accounts in the other worlds of welfare capitalism. Alain Supiot (2001) provides part of the background to this in his support notion for 'social drawing rights'. Supiot was the general rapporteur of a panel of experts convened by the European Commission in 1996 to investigate the future of work and labour law within the European Community.[1] One of the recommendations made by this policy commission concerned the extension of social drawing rights. In particular, it was noted that a certain class of rights had emerged which allowed workers to draw on credit they had earned at their workplace to do things outside their normal job. Supiot says that an example of social drawing rights can be seen in the provisions that companies make to allow employees time-off so that they can attend training courses. Supiot argues that these rights should be extended, for example to ease the transition that workers experience when they move between jobs. Supiot argues that the social element to such rights refers to the idea that such rights are established on a collective basis and are also directed at a purpose that brings benefits to society. The drawing aspect of these rights indicates that workers build up sufficient credit and then have the inclination to draw upon this reserve.

Social drawing rights provides a case for permitting people to take a break from their working lives. As a class of rights, this can be integrated into a model of citizenship. In Germany, Claus Offe (2000) provides one way that these ideas can be put into practice in his advocacy of sabbatical accounts. Offe argues that the German welfare system has been built historically around the needs of workers. This system has been guided by four main principles. He says that these principles have complex historical origins and have evolved over a considerable period of time. First, the protection of standards in employment. This protects individuals within their working environment and covers things such as limits on the working day and a ban on child labour. Second, the assistance offered to people outside their working life. For example, social security systems that protects the income of workers and their families in the event of illness. Third, the defence of collective bargaining. This provides organised labour with an important role in determining the conditions under which workers operate. Fourth, the pursuit of full employment. This generates much of the revenue needed to pay for welfare payments. Furthermore, being in employment helps ensure that people do not fall prey to problems such as poverty. A stable macroeconomic framework provides some of the conditions for full employment, for example by creating a stable and predictable environment in which firms can make investment decisions.

Claus Offe argues that this welfare system is now under strain. He says that this emerges from domestic factors such as the impact of German reunification as well as international developments such as economic globalisation. Offe says that these challenges give rise to 'precariousness' in the areas of production and distribution. Precariousness in production refers to the increased risks that people face in their working lives. He says that traditionally welfare is based on the assumption that a person will be in the same job throughout their life. Economic changes mean, however, that the 'job-for-life' is being steadily eroded. People face more irregular and unprotected employment. Precariousness in distribution concerns the shortfalls that people encounter in income, housing and health services. Offe argues that traditionally German welfare has tied together the spheres of production and distribution. Stable employment provided enough security for distribution. Offe states that this coupling of production and distribution is increasingly inadequate. The risks faced in employment do not provide sufficient guarantees in distribution.

Offe contends that the best way of dealing with both types of precariousness is to move beyond the historic emphasis on workers and embrace universal economic citizenship. Offe argues that universal economic citizenship would uncouple the spheres of production and distribution and provide rights to workers and non-workers alike. He says that one option is to use an unconditional basic income to underpin universal economic citizenship. He writes that the, 'most far-reaching alternative approach to the problems of precariousness involves strategies advocating a basic income as a universal economic citizenship (as to employee) right' (Offe 2000, 30). The basic income will not be linked to a person's current or past employment record, and so disconnects citizenship from an emphasis on work. Offe continues, however, that an unconditional basic income is unlikely to be a feasible policy option. He says that such an income is likely to be prohibitively expensive and it is hard to predict the overall consequences of such a policy on the economy. He calls for a more gradual and experimental approach. He proposes that each citizen could be born with entitlement to a sabbatical account as a condition of citizenship. He suggests that the account could cover 10 years of subsistence level income, and people could be allowed to draw on this account at any age between early adulthood (he says this could be 18) and retirement. This would permit people to take a sabbatical from their working lives, although constraints would be placed on the length of the opt-outs (he suggests six months at a time). Offe says that the sabbatical accounts would only be made available to those with a vocational training certificate or an employment record of least 3 years. He states that this would help prevent using their sabbatical accounts to avoid training. Offe proposes that diverting spending from existing social assistance or training schemes would pay for the sabbatical accounts. Claus Offe presents his argument as an attempt to implement a universal system of economic citizenship. Offe is concerned with a just system of distribution and his proposal is not geared towards the production of economic surplus. His model is not geared towards the production of economic surplus.

Interest in sabbatical accounts is not confined to the non-liberal world. For example, in Britain Linda Boyes and James McCormick examine sabbatical accounts as part of a study for the Scottish Council Foundation on 're-working time' and retirement. Boyes and McCormick (2006) explore ways that employees can be granted special leave to pursue other activities. Drawing on ideas and initiatives within Australia and Canada, Boyes and McCormick identify two models for special leave, although they say that elements of these models could be combined to form hybrid approaches. One option is to allow employees to 'bank' a fixed amount of holidays or overtime for a later date. They suggest that if a person has 25 days of annual leave, then a person might bank 5 days a year over a 5 year period so that in the 6th year they could have their normal 25 day holiday plus their 25 banked days to have 50 days leave. A different option is to allow individuals to defer part of their salary into a scheme. They highlight an initiative within the British Columbia Public Service in Canada that allows employees to defer between 10 per cent and 33 per cent of their gross salary to help pay for a period of leave of between 6 months and 1 year. To participate in this scheme, individuals have to have had at least 2 years service and defer a portion of their salary for between 1 and 6 years. Nick Pearce, Will Paxton and Stuart White (2006) argue that the common interest in sabbatical accounts across different worlds of welfare capitalism could be used to develop a policy front that has broad international appeal and could be used as a basis for discussion and co-operation among policy-makers in countries with different welfare traditions.

The third way

The above argument rejects the idea that the assets agenda is simply an Anglo-Saxon policy. This argument does not explain, however, why there is currently a strong association between the assets agenda and the Anglo-Saxon world. One possibility is that it is simply a coincidence that the assets agenda has emerged most importantly in the United States, Canada, Britain, Australia and New Zealand. This probably contains an element of truth. However, if the pattern of the assets agenda was simply random, then one would expect this agenda to have spread more extensively beyond the Anglo-Saxon world by now. The fact that this had not happened suggests that the current spread of asset ideas cannot be explained solely or mainly as a chance occurrence.

One could acknowledge instead that there is a link between the assets agenda and the Anglo-Saxon world but deny this is because assets belong to a liberal welfare agenda. I make an alternative suggestion that connects assets to the 'third way'. Since the mid-1970s, countries such as the United States, Britain, Australia and Canada have been at the forefront of neoliberal or free market ideas and policies (Holtham and Kay 1994). Neoliberalism challenged progressive ideals and policies and in particular the emphasis that was placed on the state within public policy. Part of the response of the left in these countries has been to accept these criticisms of the state but reject free market prescriptions. This has stimulated a search for a 'third way' alternative to state-centred and free market policies.

The assets agenda forms one component of the third way. Bruce Ackerman and Anne Alstott state that, 'We mean to define a third way ... Our proposal for a stakeholder society takes one large step towards this ideal' (Ackerman and Alstott 1999, 4). Some versions of asset-based welfare are compatible with free market policies. Those schemes that are voluntary, favour those who already own wealth, and are accumulated and traded through the market can be considered as being compatible with the free market. However, those versions of assets that are currently dominant have greater claim of adding to the third way. Within social policy this applies to those models that invoke a 'social investment' state (Sherraden 2003; Diamond and Giddens 2005). Anthony Giddens (1998, 2000, 2001) is one of the leading exponents of the third way. The social investment state is central to his vision of the third way. He writes that, 'In place of the welfare state we should put the *social investment state*, operating in the context of a positive welfare society ... The top-down dispensation of benefit should cede place to more localized distribution systems' (Giddens 1998, 117–118). The social investment state differs from the model of the state in post-war social democracy by placing more emphasis on empowering individuals to help themselves. The social investment state differs from free markets by envisaging an active role for the state to intervene in markets to ensure that people have access to endowments. Patrick Diamond and Anthony Giddens (2005) suggest that one strand of social investment should focus on providing assets to individuals. The citizenship wing of the assets agenda is part of a broader progressive engagement with social citizenship, although the provision of assets directly to individuals means this eschews state-centred programmes. Assets also run counter to the neoliberal hostility towards social citizenship.

The quest for a third way has been strongest in those countries with an experience of neoliberalism, perhaps because of the need to renew progressive ideals has been felt most urgently. This helps explain the association of asset policies with the Anglo-Saxon world. However, this is a contingent fact. Third way debates could have appeared more strongly elsewhere, driven by a range of factors. The third way offers a way of understanding the current pattern of asset policies without also insisting that assets are chained to the Anglo-Saxon world.

Assets and the right

Much of this book has focused on arguments emerging from the progressive wing of politics. Bruce Ackerman, Anne Alstott, Samuel Bowles, Herbert Gintis, Michael Sherraden and Stuart White all pursue a reformist agenda. This is because most of the modern interest and the most developed models, occur on the left of the political spectrum. However, interest in assets is not confined to the left. Chapter 1 noted that forerunners to assets agenda can be detected in the thought of Conservatives such as Quintin Hogg and in Margaret Thatcher's attempts to create a popular capitalism.

Today, asset-based ideas attract interest among the right in places such as the United States and Britain. In the United States, the Cato Institute displays interest in assets as part of its research into the ownership society. The Cato Institute is a policy organisation based in Washington D.C. that supports limited government, individual freedom and free markets. Individual ownership is thought to be important for promoting responsibility, prosperity and liberty. Tom Palmer (2004) argues that private property encourages people to behave responsibly. Ownership means that people bear the consequences of their actions, for good or ill. Palmer says that being held to account for one's actions encourages responsibility. Palmer continues that private ownership provides incentives for people to create value and so supports prosperity. He writes that, 'Ownership makes markets possible, and markets make prosperity possible' (Palmer 2004). David Boaz (2006) contends that individual ownership supports freedom by diffusing power and so protects individuals from encroachments from the state.

Health Service Accounts (HSAs) is one type of policy that attracts interest among the right. HSAs were established in a Medicare reform bill that was signed into law by President George Bush in December 2003. HSAs are accounts that permit individuals to make tax-free savings for medical expenses. These accounts have to be accompanied by an approved insurance plan, and individuals who receive government health benefits (such as Medicare and Medicaid) are generally not eligible for these accounts. For 2006, individuals are allowed to save up to $2,700 a year into these accounts (this figure rises to $5,450 for families). Account holders decide how to spend the money in their accounts. Three million individuals owned HSAs in January 2006, with around a third of individuals in 2005 belonging to a low or moderate income bracket (of below $50,000 a year).[2] The Cato Institute argues that HSAs should be made more flexible for Americans.[3] It suggests dropping the requirement that HSAs have to be accompanied by an insurance plan, saying that government should leave the decision about whether or not to take out insurance to the consumer. It also proposes that the annual contribution limits should be raised, and these accounts should be extended into the Medicare and Medicaid programmes.[4]

In Britain, the Conservative party backed the introduction of the Child Trust Fund. George Osborne, the current shadow chancellor, led the Conservative response when the Child Trust Fund bill was discussed before the House of Commons. In a debate on the Child Trust Fund in the House of Commons on 15 December 2003 George Osborne stated that, 'Let me make it clear from the outset that we greatly support the principle that the Bill is designed to promote. Conservative Members believe in the virtue of savings. We think that having savings, like owning one's home, gives people a stake in society, gives them independence, encourages self-reliance and bolsters the freedom of the individual against the overbearing state. In that sense, it is the most practical manifestation of liberty' (Commons Hansard, volume 415, part number 11, column 1345). The present Conservative leader David Cameron proposed an amendment to the Child Trust Fund bill that would allow parents of disabled children to access money in the account during the 18 year old lifespan as well as removing the upper £1,200 annual savings limit into these accounts. Cameron argued that both changes would respond to the particular needs of disabled children. Cameron was proud of this intervention, declaring that, 'I've done it. I've changed something. Whatever else happens from this day onwards my parliamentary career will have some meaning. My obituary – short, dull and largely unread – will have at least one significant paragraph' (Cameron 2004).

The Conservative party research department published plans for a Lifetime Savings Account. Jesse Norman and Greg Clark (2004) argue that promoting savings are important for at least two reasons.[5] First, savings furnish people with resources they need for lifecycle needs. This encompasses saving for a deposit on a house education or training, or 'rainy day' expenditures needed to help cope with financial problems. Second, savings are important for helping provide people with a stable and comfortable lifestyle in retirement. To support saving, they advocate a LiSA that would be made available to all individuals aged 18 or over. Each year, the government would match every £1 saved in the account up to a certain amount (in the document the matching rate and annual cap are put out for consultation). In an interest bearing cash version of the scheme, a person's deposit and government match earn interest at normal commercial rates. Individuals can withdraw their own contributions and the interest this accrues at any point, but they can only keep the matched savings component if the withdrawn sum is replaced quickly. They say that upon retirement, or perhaps in the event of a serious illness, people can withdraw all the money in their account. If a person dies the sums saved can be transferred to their beneficiaries. Norman and Clark state that no restrictions should be placed on how funds are spent and it would be desirable if the amounts saved in the LiSA could be ignored when working out the other benefits a person might receive from government. They add that the LiSA could be developed as a 'wrapper' that is capable of being applied to a range of financial products (such as bond, equity or cash accounts) rather than being tied to a particular product.

Assets then are not the exclusive provenance of the left. Assets cannot be described as strictly being a left wing or right wing idea. Personal responsibility and the virtues of private ownership in encouraging economic enterprise appeal to the right. The left favours the role that assets can play in overcoming wealth inequality and giving people the resources they need to realise their opportunities. Assets cut across political boundaries, and whether a particular programme appeals to the left or right depends importantly on how the programme is shaped. Much of the current interest among the right is towards social policy models. This can be seen in the emphasis in the United States and Britain on policies such as HSAs and Lifetime Savings Accounts. One of the key differences between left and right over assets concerns the treatment of inequality. Inequality of property means that redistribution may be required to secure ownership for all. Conservatives are more resistant than reformists in engaging in redistribution to secure ownership for all. Progressive commentators argue that one of the key defects of asset policies from the right is that they are regressive, favouring the asset-rich (Sherraden 2003; Kelly and Lissauer 2000). Related to this are different attitudes to the state. Reformists are more disposed than conservatives in using the state to redistribute resources from the asset-rich to the asset-poor.

Future research

Further research into the assets agenda can be shaped in a number of ways. Some suggestions are now given, although this does not outline an exhaustive list. One strand of future research might draw upon the theoretical analysis of social policy and citizenship. For example, the idea of an 'asset-effect' is crucial to models of social policy. Although there is evidence to support the existence of an asset-effect, more data is needed for more confident and robust judgements. Such a study would involve data that tracks a given set of individuals over time. John Bynner comments that, 'assessing the impact of assets on people's statuses in later adult life necessitates *longitudinal* data on the same individuals collected over an extended period of time' (Bynner 2001, 17). Such data will allow an investigation of whether the ownership of assets has an identifiable and independent effect on later welfare outcomes. It would be useful if such a dataset could include information on the Child Trust Fund as this would provide direct evidence on a particular asset policy. One could use data to track saving and welfare outcomes associated with the Child Trust Fund. A different part of this study could build on this by looking in more detail at how an asset-effect is generated. Identifying the particular aspect of asset-ownership that contributes to any asset-effect would allow policy to be better designed to promote an asset-effect. Will Paxton comments that, 'What part of the asset-experience creates positive welfare outcomes? Is it predominantly the accumulation, holding or spending of the asset and what are the implications of this for policy?' (Paxton 2001, 14).

The discussion of the different worlds of welfare capitalism suggested that the citizenship wing could be used to expand the assets ideas beyond the Anglo-Saxon world. A future project could test this suggestion. For example, a study could examine how concrete proposals for a sabbatical account could be developed in Germany or Sweden. This project could involve interviewing various policy figures (such as politicians, trade union leaders and policy researchers) about the features they want to see in a sabbatical account and how such a policy would fit alongside income benefits and public services. This could be complemented by a study of the attitudes of citizens in these countries towards different proposals for sabbatical accounts.

The original evidence reported in this book could also be the basis for further study. The focus groups on the Child Trust Fund revealed the concerns parents have with the quality of financial information they receive. This provokes a broad question about the quality of financial information and financial literacy or capability. Part of this could explore the appropriate content of financial information. This would consider how information could be presented in a simple and transparent manner. Improving financial understanding should look at the skills that people need to process information. This strand could identify the skills people need and contemplate how people acquire those skills, particularly for those who have already left school, college or university.

The focus groups on wealth taxation signalled the interest people showed in the community fund proposal. One could develop this by studying in more detail how such an idea could be fashioned into practical proposals. This could specify in depth the ways that the initial funds could be raised; examine the particular schemes that such a fund could be used for; and study how the delegation of the fund to the private sector would operate in practice.

Notes

1 Introduction

1. Reported on http://www.whitehouse.gov/news/releases/2004/09/20040902-2. html, accessed 1/3/07.
2. Reported on http://www.australianpolitics.com/news/2003/09/03-09-21.shtml, accessed 1/3/07.
3. Noted on, http://www.weforum.org/en/knowledge/KN_SESS_SUMM_ 11208?url=/en/knowledge/KN_SESS_SUMM_11208, accessed 1/3/07.
4. More recently, John Hills (2007) shows interest in allowing people to build up equity stakes in a report on social housing in England. Hills argues that those living in social housing often display a significant level of dissatisfaction with their homes. This unhappiness stems in part from a lack of control people feel over their homes. Hills suggests that one way of trying to avert this dissatisfaction is to give tenants a sense of ownership by allowing them to build up an equity stake in their own homes.
5. Samuel Brittan and Barry Riley (1978) also provide an early model of capital grants in their proposal to use revenues derived from North Sea oil to provide capital stakes for all. *Financial Times* journalist Samuel Brittan is one of the most prominent and long-standing supporters of capital grants in the mainstream press (Brittan 2001; 2003).

2 Social Policy

1. An emphasis on independence does not attract universal support. Richard Sennett (2003) argues that compassion should be central to welfare policy, but that pursuing independence implies care without compassion. He argues that dependency is a good thing in welfare policy because it embodies a positive relationship between a carer and a dependant, with a carer providing help on the basis of respect and compassion. Sennett says that while the value of dependency within families is often recognised, in the public sphere it is usually frowned upon. He notes, 'In private life, dependence ties people together. A child who could not depend on adults for guidance would be a profoundly damaged human being, unable to learn, deeply insecure ... In the public realm, however, dependence appears shameful' (Sennett 2003, 101). Sennett argues that the concern in public life is driven by an 'infantilization thesis', that is stressing dependence will make adults behave like children. He criticises capital grant proposals such as the Child Trust Fund because it minimises the, 'subjective sides of the welfare state – for there is no longer "welfare" as a

face-to-face human interaction. The gift is no longer a personal gift; you would have to thank the Treasury's computers' (Sennett 2003, 141).

Two things might be said in reply to this critique. First, dependency carries costs as well as benefits. A situation in which a person is completely dependent upon another makes the dependant vulnerable to exploitation. A carer could ignore the wishes or needs of an dependant. Sennett acknowledges this possibility when he says that students taught by commands or patients that do not receive any information from their doctor become, 'spectators to their own needs worked upon by a superior power' (Sennett 2003, 106). Thus, even if dependence should be a feature of welfare policy, there also ought to be room for independence. Insofar as assets help guarantee this independence, they could be a valuable policy tool. Second, independence need not signal lack of compassion. Resources may be provided so that they can become independent on the basis of compassion, that is on the belief that all should have access to those things that allow them to shape their life in the direction of their choices. Even if one believes the value of independence is overstated and dependence ignored this does not mean that independence should play no role at all in welfare policy.

3   Citizenship

1. Bruce Ackerman and Anne Alstott say in their book that they see themselves as part of an American republican tradition. Although Ackerman and Alstott describe themselves as republicans, on the understanding of republicanism used in my book (which involves some requirement to act or behave in particular ways) they are better categorised as liberals.
2. Ackerman and Alstott also suggest denying grants to those that have a serious criminal record. They argue that the threat of withdrawing the $80,000 stake is a powerful economic deterrent from committing serious crime. The stakeholder grant can therefore be used as a way of stemming criminal activity.

5   The Child Trust Fund

1. Elaine Kempson, Adele Atkinson and Sharon Collard (2006) provide more evidence on the Child Trust Fund and saving in a report conducted for Her Majesty's Revenue and Customs. This report looked at the level and nature of saving prior to the introduction of the Child Trust Fund and intended savings into this policy. This involved a survey of 1,071 parents who are eligible for the Child Trust Fund (which was weighted to provide a sample of 500 individuals). These parents were asked how much they expected to save into these accounts. Kempson, Atkinson and Collard found that around three quarters of respondents thought that they would add to the CTF accounts, although roughly half thought they would do

so over the coming year. The median amount that was expected to be added over the coming year was £240. Overall, Kempson, Atkinson and Collard conclude that if parents fulfilled their expectations, then the Child Trust Fund would increase the level of savings for children.

6   Paying for Assets

1. Reported on http://news.bbc.co.uk/1/hi/health/6157219.stm, accessed on 5/3/07.

7   Conclusion

1. The members of the expert group were: María Emilia Casas (Complutense University of Madrid); Jean De Munck (Louvain University, College Thomas More), Peter Hanau (Cologne University), Anders Johansson (National Institute of Economic and Social Research, Stockholm), Pamela Meadows (National Institute of Economic and Social Research), Enzo Mingione (Padua University), Robert Salais (Laboratory 'Institutions et Dynamiques Historiques de l'Economie', CNRS-Ecole Normale Supérieure de Cachan), Alain Supiot (Nantes University, Wissenschaftskolleg du Berlin) and Paul van der Heijden (Amsterdam University).
2. Reported at www.whitehouse.gov/news/releases/2006/04/print/20060405-6. html, accessed on 16/2/07.
3. At www.cato.org/special/ownership_society/healthcare2.html, accessed 16/2/07.
4. See Paul Krugman and Robin Wells (2006) for a critique of HSAs. Krugman and Wells argue that the tax breaks associated with HSAs favour the rich; that people are often not capable of making informed choices about medical matters; and that HSAs may help unravel employer-based medical insurance through an 'adverse selection' problem. In particular, healthier individuals are more likely to opt out of employer-based insurance and take-out this policy. This leaves less healthy people remaining within employer-based insurance, and this will put pressure on insurers to raise premiums (Krugman and Wells 2006).

   These criticisms need not apply to all models of HSAs. Progressives often complain that the asset policies pursued by the right are regressive in nature. Presumably, it is possible to develop models of HSAs that eliminates tax breaks for the rich. Making HSAs compulsory rather than voluntary may mitigate the adverse selection problem. The evidence collected in the focus groups on the Child Trust Fund indicates that the capability of individuals to deploy assets is a legitimate issue. However, the focus group sessions do not suggest that people are incapable of processing information. Whether the difficulties people encounter are much greater in health and that these barriers render HSAs inoperable is open to debate.

5. Jesse Norman has since become a director of Policy Exchange, a think-tank with close affiliations to the present Conservative leadership. Greg Clark was elected a Conservative Member of Parliament in 2005, and served on the party's Social Justice policy commission. An interim report of this group shows interest in asset-based welfare (Clark 2006).

References

Ackerman, B., Alstott, A. and Van Parijs, P. (2005) *Redesigning Distribution: basic income and stakeholder grants as cornerstones for an egalitarian capitalism* (London: Verso).

Ackerman, B. (2003) 'Radical liberalism', in Dowding, K., De Wispelaere, J. and White, S. (eds) *The Ethics of Stakeholding* (Basingstoke: Palgrave Macmillan), 170–189.

Ackerman, B. and Alstott, A. (1999) *The Stakeholder Society* (New Haven: Yale University Press).

Ackerman, B. (1980) *Social Justice in a Liberal State* (New Haven: Yale University Press).

Allen Consulting Group (2003) *Asset Based Policies, Matched Savings Accounts: exploring options* (Canberra: Allen Consulting Group Limited).

Alstott, A. (2004) *No Exit: what parents owe their children and what society owes parents* (New York: Oxford University Press).

Anderson, E. (1999) 'What is the point of equality?', *Ethics*, 109(2), 287–337.

Appelby, J. and Ball, T. (ed.) (1999) *Jefferson: Political Writings* (Cambridge: Cambridge University Press).

Atkinson, A.B. (1972) *Unequal Shares: wealth in Britain* (London: Penguin Press).

Barnard, H. and Pettigrew, N. (2003) *Tenant and Other Stakeholders' Attitudes Towards Housing Equity Stakes* (London: Office of the Deputy Prime Minister).

Barnes, M. (2002) 'Reaching the socially excluded?', in Kober, C. and Paxton, W. (ed.) *Asset-based Welfare and Poverty: exploring the case for and against asset-based welfare policies* (London: Institute for Public Policy Research and End Child Poverty), 13–16.

Belloc, H. (1927) [1913] *The Servile State* (London: Constable and Company Limited).

Berlin, I. (1958) *Two Concepts of Liberty* (Oxford: Clarendon).

Blank, R. and Burua, V. (2004) *Comparative Health Policy* (Basingstoke: Palgrave).

Bloor, M., Frankland, J., Thomas, M. and Robson, K. (2001) *Focus Groups in Social Research* (Sage: Thousand Oaks).

Blunkett, D. (2005) *The Asset State: the future of welfare*, reprinted at http://www.ippr.org.uk/events/?id=1529, accessed on 26/7/05.

Blunkett, D. (2001) *Politics and Progress: renewing democracy and civil society* (London: Demos and Politicos).

Boaz, D. (2006) *Defining an ownership society*, www.cato.org/special/ownership_society/boaz.html, accessed 16/2/07.

Bowles, S., Gintis, H. and Osborne Groves, M. (eds) (2005) *Unequal Chances. Family background and economic success* (New York: Russell Sage Foundation).

Bowles, S. and Gintis, H. (1998) 'Efficient redistribution: new rules for markets, states and communities', in Wright, E.O. (ed.) *Recasting Egalitarianism: new rules for communities, states and markets* (New York: Verso), 3–71.

Boyes, L. and McCormick, J. (2006) 'Having the time for our life: re-working time', in Paxton, W., White, S. and Maxwell, D. (eds) *The Citizen's Stake: exploring the future of universal asset policies* (Bristol: Policy Press), 165–176.

Brittan, S. (2003) 'The Logic of the Baby Bond', *Prospect*, August, reproduced at http://www.samuelbrittan.co.uk/text159_p.html, accessed 27/2/07.

Brittan, S. (2001) 'In praise of Brown's Trust Fund', *Financial Times*, 24 May, reproduced at http://www.samuelbrittan.co.uk/text78_p.html, accessed 27/2/07.

Brittan, S. and Riley, B. (1978) *A People's Stake in North Sea Oil* (Manchester Statistical Society: Manchester).

Bush, G.W. (2004) *President's remarks at the 2004 Republican national convention*, at http://www.whitehouse.gov/news/releases/2004/09/print/20040902-2.html

Bynner, J. (2001) 'The effects of assets on life chances', in Bynner, J. and Paxton, W., *The Asset-Effect* (London: Institute for Public Policy Research), 17–37.

Bynner, J. and Despotidou, S. (2001) *The Effect of Assets on Life Chances* (London: Institute of Education), reprinted at http://www.cesi.org.uk/kbdocs/assets.doc (accessed on 29/05/07).

Cameron, D. (2004) 'Cameron's Law', *The Guardian*, 19 January.

Cheng, L. (2007) *Asset-based Policy in Taiwan: demonstrations and policy progress*, http://gwbweb.wustl.edu/csd/Publications/2007/Taiwan_Update_2007_01_15.pdf, accessed 1/3/07.

Chowa, G. (2007) *Asset Building in Sub-Saharan Africa: toward sustainable economic development for rural farmers*, at http://gwbweb.wustl.edu/csd/Publications/2007/Africa_Update_2007_01_17.pdf, accessed 1/3/07.

Clark, G. (2006) *The Anatomy of Poverty*, at www.socialjusticechallenge.com/fileadmin/user_upload/socialjustice/the_anatomy_of_poverty.pdf

Clark, H. (2005) *Statement to Parliament*, reprinted on http://www.beehive.govt.nz/ViewDocument.aspx?DocumentID=22087, accessed on 2/10/06.

Commission on Life Chances and Child Poverty (2006) *Narrowing the Gap: the final report of the Fabian Commission on Life Chances and Child Poverty* (London: The Fabian Society).

Commission on Social Justice (1994) *Social Justice: strategies for national renewal*, (London: Vintage).

Commission on Taxation and Citizenship (2000) *Paying for Progress: a new politics of tax for public spending* (London: The Fabian Society).

Cunliffe, J. and Erreygers, G. (2004) (ed.) *The Origins of Universal Grants. An anthology of historical writings on basic capital and basic income* (Basingstoke: Palgrave Macmillan).

Cunliffe, J. and Erreygers, G. (2003) 'Basic Income? Basic Capital! Origins and Issues of a Debate', *Journal of Political Philosophy*, 11(1), 89–110.

Davey, E. (2006) *Child Trust Fund May Increase Rather Than Decrease Inequality*, (www.libdems.org.uk/news/child-trust-fund-may-increase-rather-than-decrease-inequality-davey.html), accessed 14/02/06.

Diamond, P. and Giddens, A. (2005) 'The new egalitarianism: economic inequality in the UK', in Giddens, A. and Diamond, P. (ed.) *The New Egalitarianism* (Cambridge: Polity), 101–119.

Dobson, A. (2004) *Citizenship and the Environment* (Oxford: Oxford University Press).

Dowding, K., De Wispelaere, J. and White, S. (eds) (2003) *The Ethics of Stakeholding* (Basingstoke: Palgrave Macmillan).

Edwards, L. (2000) *Assets Focus Groups: topline findings* (London: Institute for Public Policy Research).

Edwards, L. (2001) *Equity Stakes, Fair Stakes?: key findings from focus group research with council and housing association tenants* (London: Institute for Public Policy Research).

Emmerson, C. and Wakefield, M. (2003) 'Increasing support for those on lower incomes: is the Saving Gateway the best policy response?', *Fiscal Studies*, 24(2), 167–195.

Emmerson, C. and Wakefield, M. (2001) *The Saving Gateway and the Child Trust Fund: is asset-based welfare 'well fair'?* (London: Institute for Fiscal Studies).

Esping-Andersen, G. (2004) [1990] *Three Worlds of Welfare Capitalism* (Cambridge: Polity).

Esping-Andersen, G. (2002) 'Towards the good society, once again?', in Esping-Andersen, G., Gallie, D., Hemerijck, A. and Myles, D., *Why We Need a New Welfare State* (Oxford: Oxford University Press), 1–25.

Fabre, C. (2003) 'The Stake: an egalitarian proposal?', in Dowding, K., De Wispelaere, J. and White, S. (eds) *The Ethics of Stakeholding* (Basingstoke: Palgrave Macmillan), 114–129.

Field, F. (2000) *The State of Dependency: welfare under Labour* (London: Social Market Foundation).

Field, F. (ed.) (1996) *Stakeholder Welfare* (London: Institute of Economic Affairs).

Finlayson, A. (forthcoming) 'Characterising New Labour: the case of the Child Trust Fund', *Public Administration*.

Fitzpatrick, T. (1999) *Freedom and Security: an introduction to the basic income debate* (Basingstoke: Macmillan).

Fölster, S. (2001) 'Asset-based social insurance in Sweden', in Regan, S. and Paxton, W. (ed.) *Asset-based Welfare: international experiences* (London: Institute for Public Policy Research), 74–83.

Fölster, S., Gidehag, R., Orszag, M. and Snower, D.J. (2003) 'Assessing the effect of introducing welfare accounts in Sweden', in Andersen, T.M. and Molander, P. (ed.) *Alternatives for Welfare Policy. Coping with Internationalisation and Demographic Change* (Cambridge: Cambridge University Press), 350–375.

Gamble, A. and Prabhakar, R. (2006) 'Assets and Capital Grants: the attitudes of young people towards capital grants', in Paxton, W. and White, S. (eds) *The New Politics of Ownership* (Bristol: Policy Press), 107–119.

Gamble, A. and Wright. T. (2004) 'Introduction', in Gamble, A. and Wright, T. (eds) *Restating the State?* (Oxford: Blackwell in association with the *Political Quarterly*), 1–10.

George, H. (1932) [1879] *Progress and Poverty: an inquiry into the cause of material depressions and of increase of want with increase of wealth* (London: Vacher and Sons Limited).

Giddens, A. (2001) *The Global Third Way Debate* (Cambridge: Polity).

Giddens, A. (2000) *The Third Way and its Critics* (Cambridge: Polity).

Giddens, A. (1998) *The Third Way: the renewal of social democracy* (Cambridge: Polity).

Glennerster, H. and McKnight, A. (2006) 'A capital start: but how far do we go?', in Paxton, W., White, S. and Maxwell, D. (ed.) *The Citizen's Stake: exploring the future of universal asset policies* (Bristol: Policy Press), 87–103.

Goodin, R.E. (2003) 'Sneaking up on stakeholding', in Dowding, K., De Wispelaere, J. and White, S. (eds) *The Ethics of Stakeholding* (Basingstoke: Palgrave Macmillan), 65–78.

Graetz, M.J. and Shapiro, I. (2005) *Death by a Thousand Cuts: the fight over taxing inherited wealth* (New Jersey: Princeton University Press).

Gray, J. (2000) *Two Faces of Liberalism* (Cambridge: Polity).

Haveman, R. (1988) *Starting Even: an equal opportunity program to combat the nation's new poverty* (New York: Simon and Schuster).

Hedges, A. and Bromley, C. (2001) *Public Attitudes Towards Taxation: the report of research conducted for the Fabian Commission on Taxation and Citizenship* (London: The Fabian Society).

Her Majesty's Treasury (2001a) *Savings and Assets for All: the modernisation of Britain's tax and benefit system number 8* (London: Her Majesty's Treasury).

Her Majesty's Treasury (2001b) *Delivering Savings and Assets: the modernisation of Britain's tax and benefit system number 9* (London: Her Majesty's Treasury).

Her Majesty's Treasury (2003) *Detailed Proposals for the Child Trust Fund* (London: The Stationary Office).

Her Majesty's Treasury (2004) *Opportunity for all: The strength to take the long-term decisions for Britain* (London: The Stationary Office).

Her Majesty's Treasury (2006) *A Strong and Strengthening Economy: investing in Britain's future* (London: Her Majesty's Stationary Office).

Hills, J. (2007) *Ends and Means: the future roles of social housing in England*, http://stircerd.lse.ac.uk/dps/case/cr/CASEreport34.pdf, accessed 1/3/07.

Hogg, Q. (1947) *The Case for Conservatism* (West Drayton: Penguin).

Kelly, G. and Lissauer, R. (2000) *Ownership for All* (London: Institute for Public Policy Research).

Holtham, G. (1999) 'Ownership and social democracy', in Gamble, A. and Wright, T. (eds) *The New Social Democracy* (Oxford: Blackwell), 53–68.

Holtham, G. and Kay, J. (1994) 'The Assessment: institutions of policy', *Oxford Review of Economic Policy*, 10(3), 1–16.

Kaufman, A. (2004) 'Choice, responsibility and equality', *Political Studies*, 52(4), 819–836.

Kelly, G. and Gamble, A. (1996) 'The politics of ownership', *New Left Review*, 220 (Nov/Dec), pp. 62–97.

Kelly, G. and Lissauer, R. (2000) *Ownership for All* (London: Institute for Public Policy Research).

Kempson, E., Atkinson, A. and Collard, S. (2006) *Saving for Children: a baseline survey at the inception of the Child Trust Fund*, available at http://www.pfrc.bris.ac.uk/publications/pensions_savings/Reports/Saving_for_children_report.pdf, accessed on 30/10/2006.

Kempson, E., McKay, S. and Collard, S. (2005) *Incentives to Save: Encouraging Saving Among Low-Income Households. Final Report on the Saving Gateway Pilot* (Bristol: Personal Finance Research Centre, University of Bristol).

Kreuger, R. (1994) *Focus Groups: a practical guide for applied research* (Newbury Park: Sage).

Krugman, P. and Wells, R. (2006) 'The health crisis and what to do about it', *New York Review of Books*, 53(5), March 23.

Labour party (2001) *Ambitions for Britain* (London: Labour Party).

Lakoff, G. (2004) *Don't Think of an Elephant! Know your values and frame the debate* (White River Junction, Vermont: Chelsea Green Publishing).

Latham, M. (2002) 'Economic Ownership – expanding the winner's circle', in Kober, C. and Paxton, W. (ed.) *Asset-based Welfare and Poverty: exploring the case for and against asset-based welfare policies* (London: Institute for Public Policy Research and End Child Poverty), 1–4.

Le Grand, J. (2003) *Motivation, Agency and Public Policy: of knights & knaves, pawns & queens* (Oxford: Oxford University Press).

Le Grand, J. (1989) 'Markets, Welfare and Equality', in Estrin, S. and Le Grand, J. (ed.) (1989) *Market Socialism* (Oxford: Clarendon), 193–211.

Le Grand, J. and Nissan, D. (2000) *A Capital Idea: start-up grants for young people* (London: Fabian Society).

Le Grand, J. and Nissan, D. (2003) 'A Capital Idea: helping the young to help themselves', in Dowding (eds) *The Ethics of Stakeholding* (Basingstoke: Palgrave Macmillan) 29–41.

Lewis, J. (2006) 'Carework: are care accounts the answer?', in Paxton, W., White, S. and Maxwell, D. (ed.) *The Citizen's Stake: exploring the future of universal asset policies* (Bristol: Policy Press), 151–164.

Lewis, M. and White, S. (2006) 'Inheritance tax: what do people think? Evidence from deliberative workshops', in Paxton, W., White, S. and Maxwell, D. (ed.) *The Citizen's Stake: exploring the future of universal asset policies* (Bristol: Policy Press), 15–35.

Liberal Democrats (2005) *The Real Alternative* (London: Liberal Democrats).

Lister, R. (1997) *Citizenship: feminist perspectives* (Basingstoke: Palgrave).

Lister, R. and Sodha, S. (2006) *The Saving Gateway: from principles to practice* (London: Institute for Public Policy Research).

Marshall, T.H. (1950) 'Citizenship and Social Class', in Marshall, T.H. and Bottomore, T. (1992) *Citizenship and Social Class* (London: Pluto Press), 3–51.

Marshall, P. (2004) 'Pension reform: a new settlement for a new century', in Marshall, P. and Laws, D. (eds) *The Orange Book: reclaiming liberalism* (London: Profile), 276–302.

Maxwell, D. (2004) *Fair Dues. Towards a More Progressive Inheritance Tax* (London: Institute for Public Policy Research).

Maxwell, D. and Sodha, S. (2006) *Turning on the Taps: next steps for CTFs*, paper presented to Political Studies Association's annual conference at the University of Reading on 6 April.

Maxwell, D. and Vigor, A. (ed.) (2005) *Time for Land Value Tax?* (London: Institute for Public Policy Research).

McKay, S. and Kempson, E. (2003) *Savings and Life Events*, research report number 194 (London: Department for Work and Pensions), 1–88.

McLean, I. (2006a) 'Land tax: options for reform', in Paxton, W., White, S. and Maxwell, D. (ed.) (2006) *The Citizen's Stake: exploring the future of universal asset policies* (Bristol: Policy Press), 69–85.

McLean, I. (2006b) *The Case for Land Value Taxation*, Compass Thinkpiece number 2, www.compassonline.org.uk/uploads/documents/CTP2TheCase ForLandValueTaxationIainMcLean.doc (accessed 10/3/2006).

Meade, J.E. (1989) *Agathopia: the economics of partnership* (Aberdeen: Aberdeen University Press).

Milburn, A. (2003) 'Assets for All', *The Guardian*, November 10.

Miller, D. (2000) *Citizenship and National Identity* (Cambridge: Polity).

Mills, G., Patterson, R., Orr, L. and DeMarco (2004) *Evaluation of the American Dream Demonstration: final evaluation report* (Cambridge, Massachusetts: Abt Associates Incorporated).

Morgan, D.L. (1997) *Focus Groups as Qualitative Research* (London: Sage).

Moury, Y. (2006) Asset-based Initiatives in Peru and Columbia: pilot study and discussion, http://gwbweb.wustl.edu/csd/Publications/2006/Peru_Update_8-10-06.pdf, accessed 1/3/07.

Nares, P. (2003) 'Creating assets for poorest among us', *The Toronto Star*, June 20.

Norman, J. and Clark, G. (2004) *Towards a Lifetime of Saving* (London: Policy Unit, Conservative Research Department).

Offe, C. (2000) 'The German Welfare State; principles, performance and perspective after unification', *Thesis Eleven*, 63(1), 11–37.

Paine, T. (1987) [1795] 'Agrarian justice', in Foot, M. and Kramnick, I. (eds) *The Thomas Paine Reader* (London: Penguin).

Palmer, T. (2004) *Great thinkers on how an ownership society fosters responsibility, liberty, prosperity*, www.cato.org/special/ownership_society/philosophy.html, accessed 16/2/07.

Pateman, C. (2004) 'Democratizing citizenship: some advantages of a basic income', *Politics and Society*, 32(1), 89–105.

Pateman, C. (2003) 'Freedom and democratization: why basic income is to be preferred to basic capital', in Dowding, K., De Wispelaere, J. and White, S. (eds) *The Ethics of Stakeholding* (Basingstoke: Palgrave Macmillan), 130–148.

Paxton, W. and White, S. (2006) 'Universal Capital Grants: the issue of responsible use', in Paxton, W., White, S. and Maxwell, D. (eds) *The Citizen's Stake: exploring the future of universal asset policies* (Bristol: Policy Press), 121–134.

Paxton, W., White, S. and Maxwell, D. (ed.) (2006), *The Citizen's Stake: exploring the future of universal asset policies* (Bristol: Policy Press).

Paxton, W. (2003) 'Introduction', in Paxton, W. (ed.) *Equal Shares? Building a progressive and coherent asset-based welfare policy* (London: Institute for Public Policy Research), 1–8.

Paxton, W. (2001) 'The Asset-Effect: an overview', in J. Bynner and W. Paxton, *The Asset-Effect* (London: Institute for Public Policy Research), 1–16.

Pearce, N., Paxton, W. and White, S. (2006) 'Conclusion: what is the best way forward for the citizen's stake', in Paxton, W., White, S. and Maxwell, D. (ed) *The Citizen's Stake: exploring the future of universal asset policies* (Bristol: Policy Press), 177–191.

Piñera, J. (1996) *Empowering Workers: the privatization of social security in Chile*, www.cato.org/pubs/journal/cj15n2-3-1.html, accessed 16/02/07.

Plender, J. (1997) *A Stake in the Future: the stakeholding solution* (London: Nicholas Brearly).

Prabhakar, R. (2006) *Rethinking Public Services* (Basingstoke: Palgrave Macmillan).

Rowlingson, K. and McKay S. (2005) *Attitudes to Inheritance in Britain* (Bristol: The Policy Press).

Schreiner, M., Clancy, M., Sherraden, M. (2002) *Final Report. Saving performance in the American Dream Demonstration. A national demonstration of Individual Development Accounts* (St Louis: Center for Social Development).

Sennett, R. (2003) *Respect: the formation of character in a world of inequality* (London: Allen Lane).

Sherraden, M. (2003) 'Assets and the Social Investment State', Paxton, W. (ed.) *Equal Shares? Building a progressive and coherent asset-based welfare policy* (London: Institute for Public Policy Research), 28–41.

Sherraden, M. (2002) *Individual Development Accounts: summary of research* (St Louis: Center for Social Development, University of Washington).

Sherraden, M. (1991) *Assets and the Poor, A New American Welfare Policy* (New York: Sharpe Incorporated).

Sherraden, M. and Zou, L. (2007) *Asset-based Policy in Hong-Kong: plans for a Child Development Fund*, http://gwbweb.wustl.edu/csd/Publications/2007/HK_Update_2007_01_06.pdf, accessed 1/3/07.

Sherraden, M. and Zou, L. (2006) *Asset-based Policy in Indonesia: pilot study and emerging opportunities*, http://gwbweb.wustl.edu/csd/Publications/2006/Indonesia_Update_4-06.pdf, accessed 1/3/07.

Shonfield, A. (1965) *Modern capitalism: the changing balance of public and private power* (New York: Oxford University Press).

Skilling, D. (2005a) *Opportunity for a Lifetime: creating an ownership society in New Zealand* (Auckland: New Zealand).

Skilling, D. (2005b) *Home Is Where the Money Is: the economic importance of saving* (Auckland: New Zealand).

Skilling, D. (2004) *It's Not Just Where The Money Is: the benefits of asset-ownership* (Auckland: New Zealand).

Stedman Jones, G. (2004) *An End to Poverty? A historical debate* (Profile: London).

Stiglitz, J.E. and Weiss, A. (1981) 'Credit rationing in markets with imperfect information', *American Economic Review*, 71(3), 393–410.

Supiot, A. (2001) *Beyond Employment. Changes in Work and the Future of Labour Law in Europe* (Oxford: Oxford University Press).

White, S. (2002) 'Must liberty and equality conflict?', *Renewal* 10(1), 27–38.

White, S. (2003) *The Civic Minimum: on the rights and obligations of economic citizenship* (Oxford: Oxford University Press).

White, S. (2006a) *Assets*, Compass thinkpiece number 12, at http://clients.squareeye.com/uploads/compass/ctp12assetsstuartwhite.pdf, accessed on 1/9/06.

White, S. (2006b) *Rawls, Republicanism and Property-Owning Democracy*, paper presented at Political Studies Association conference at the University of Reading, April 6.

Wilcox, C. (2005) 'Land Value Taxation: an economically efficient way to distribute wealth', *Renewal*, 13(4), 73–78.

Willetts, D. (2002) *Savings Revolution*, at www.davidwilletts.org.uk/record.jsp?type=article&ID=14&sectionID=2, accessed 1/3/07.

Wolff, E. (2001) 'Recent trends in wealth ownership, from 1983 to 1998', in Shapiro, T.M. and Wolff, E. (eds) *Assets for the Poor: the benefits of spreading asset ownership* (New York: Russell Sage Foundation), 34–73.

Wolff, E. (2002) *Top Heavy: the increasing inequality of wealth in America and what can be done about it* (New York: The New Press).

Index